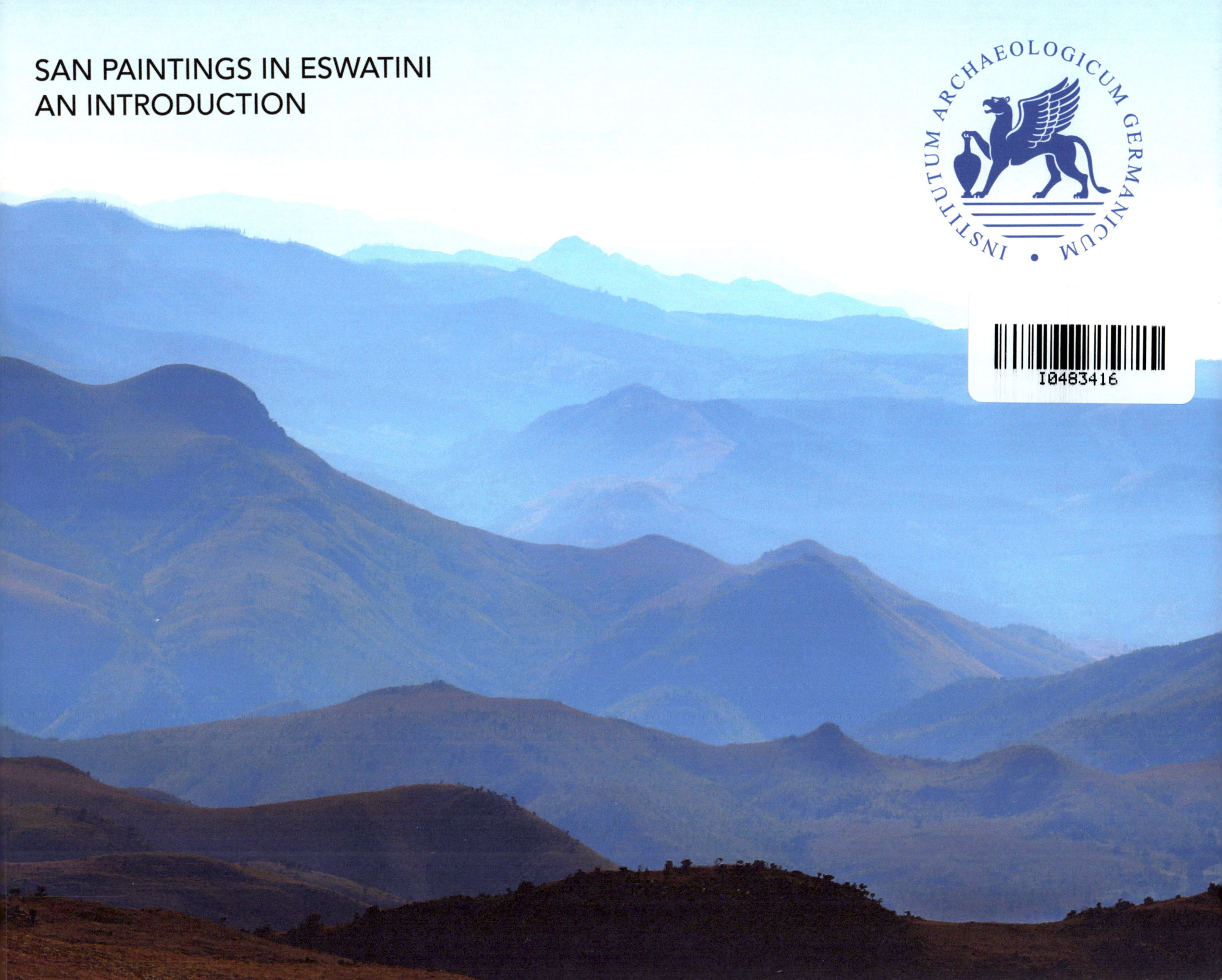

SAN PAINTINGS IN ESWATINI
AN INTRODUCTION

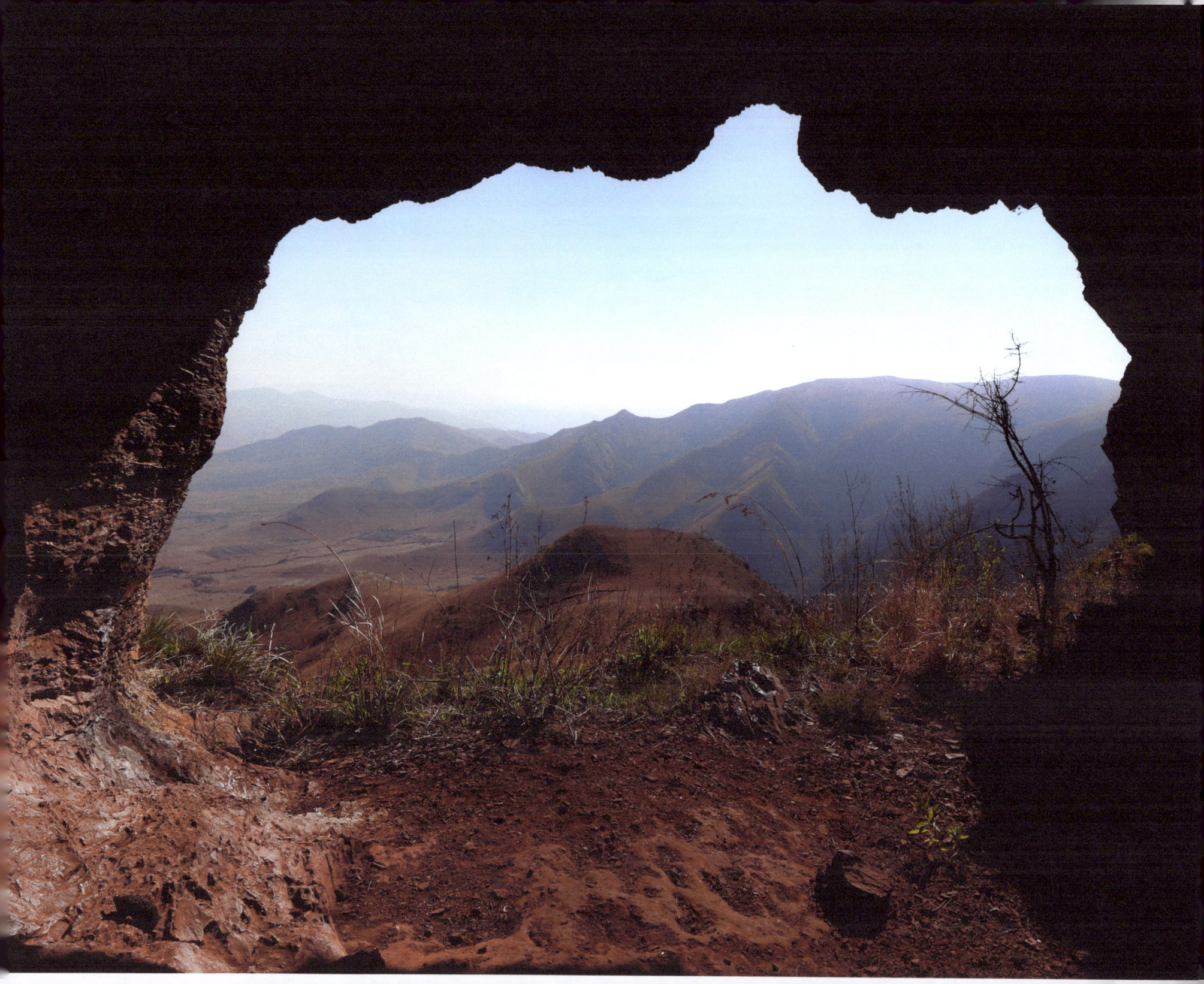

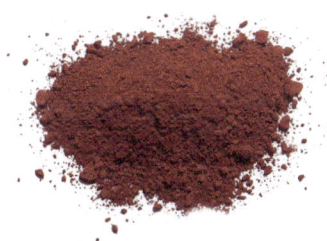

OCHRE

Chemically, ochre is oxidised iron - rust. Ochre dating back many thousands of years is found worldwide in caves, burials and was used to create rock art. Despite being so widespread, it had few practical uses in the stone ages - possibly boosting iron levels in pregnancy and for curing animal hides. It was used in composite glues to attach spear and arrow heads to wooden shafts. This does not explain why so much ochre was mined and used worldwide for so long.

Why ochre was used so intensively has been a mystery, but now archaeologists are beginning to unravel the cultural uses of ochre by early people. This book explores ancient mindsets, helping to explain why people climbed high mountain peaks to mine ochre tens of thousands of years ago - and still do so today.

ANCIENT MINES

In the 1960s, geologists came across three ancient ochre mines in Eswatini. No one knew who had made them, why ochre had been mined, or how old they were. Archaeologists were called in to help solve the puzzle. The mines were excavated when the relatively new technique of carbon dating was creating evidence based timelines around the world. For the first archaeologists could obtain credible dates for remains rich in carbon, including human and animal bones. When the results from the Swati mines came back the archaeologists were astounded - Lion Cavern was the world's most ancient mine: 43 000 years old.

Left: Inside Banda Cavern looking over Malolotja Nature Reserve.
Right: Ochre may have been rubbed on the skin for ritual use, cosmetic purposes and as sun protection.

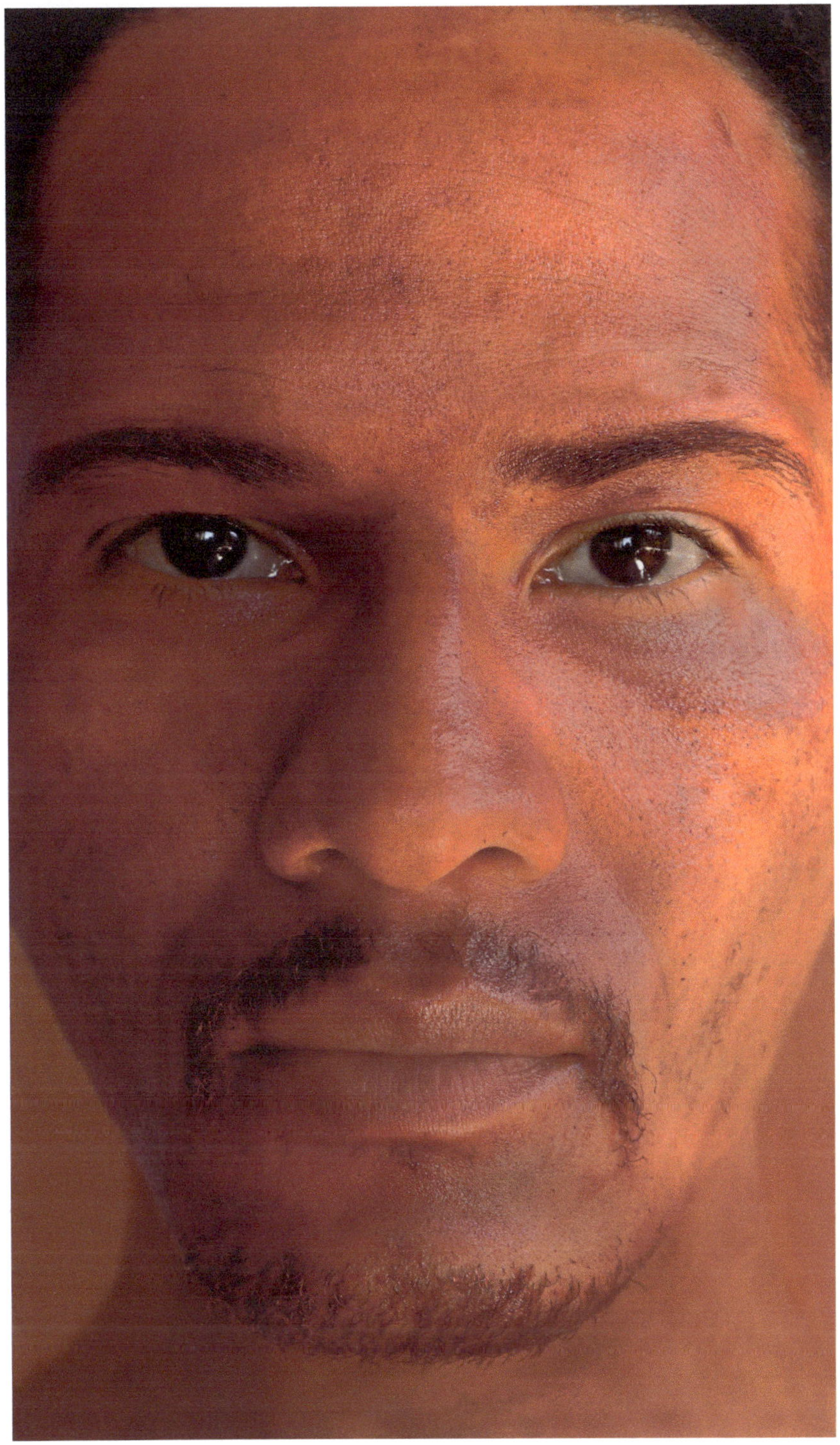

THE SAN

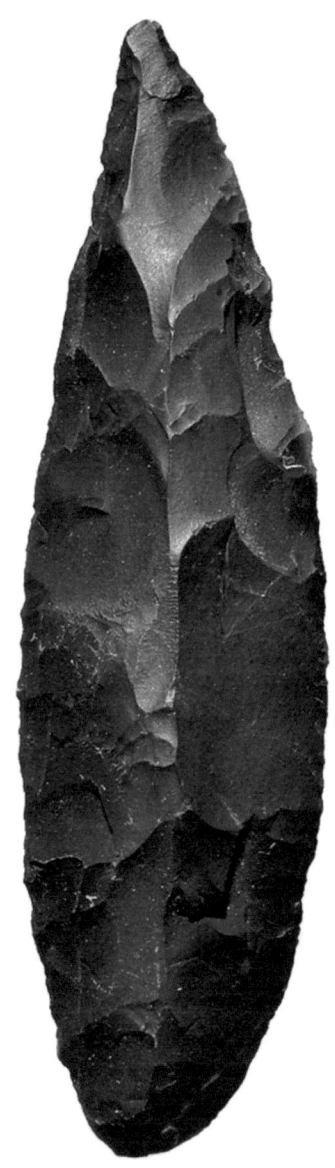

Today the San are an iconic component of southern African culture. Their tracking skills are legendary and their hunter-gatherer way of life has been carefully studied. Tiny versions of their paintings are sold on inappropriate products at almost every tourist shop south of the Zambezi.

Their culture has been romanticised. It has also been used to unite people; they are quintessentially African, yet have no political or economic power. The South African national coat of arms motto is in a Khoisan language, !Xam, and two San figures greet one another on the central shield.

We do know from analysing mitochondrial DNA that there is more genetic variation between San groups than there is between any other groups worldwide. Probably, the ancestral San were a distinct group around 100 000 years ago, long before the African exodus which peopled the world around 65 000 years ago.

Despite the great antiquity of San genetics, there is academic debate about when one can first identify San culture. Some researchers believe that this is possible just over 40 000 years ago, others that this is only possible for the last 20 000 years or less. Ancestral San would have been in Eswatini at the time when the ancient mines at Ngwenya were first being used. San used ochre extensively in their paintings. If we can understand why, then this could be a guide as to ochre's much earlier uses tens of thousands of years ago.

There were undoubtedly much earlier groups of people in Eswatini. Some created finely made stone tools like the spearpoint on the left. However, we know little about their cultures and how they perceived the world.

In comparison, San culture has been extensively recorded from the 1950s onwards, at a time when there were still San living a totally nomadic hunter-gatherer lifestyle in the Kalahari. Anthropologists studied them over generations before their nomadic lifestyle was affected by globalisation. Today there are no San who lead a completely traditional lifestyle, though many hunt and gather for long periods.

In the 1970s, around six thousand pages of Khoisan legends, gathered in the late 1800s, were translated from High Dutch into English. These provided clues as to what the paintings mean - none of the San groups today paint and they are unable to give detailed explanations of existing paintings. The result of decades of intensive research is a substantial literature on San spiritual beliefs, hunting techniques, social dynamics and ecology.

Above: A chert spearpoint found near Ngwenya Mine, stylistically dated to between 50 000 and 75 000 years old. Opposite: A contemporary San hunter from Namibia.

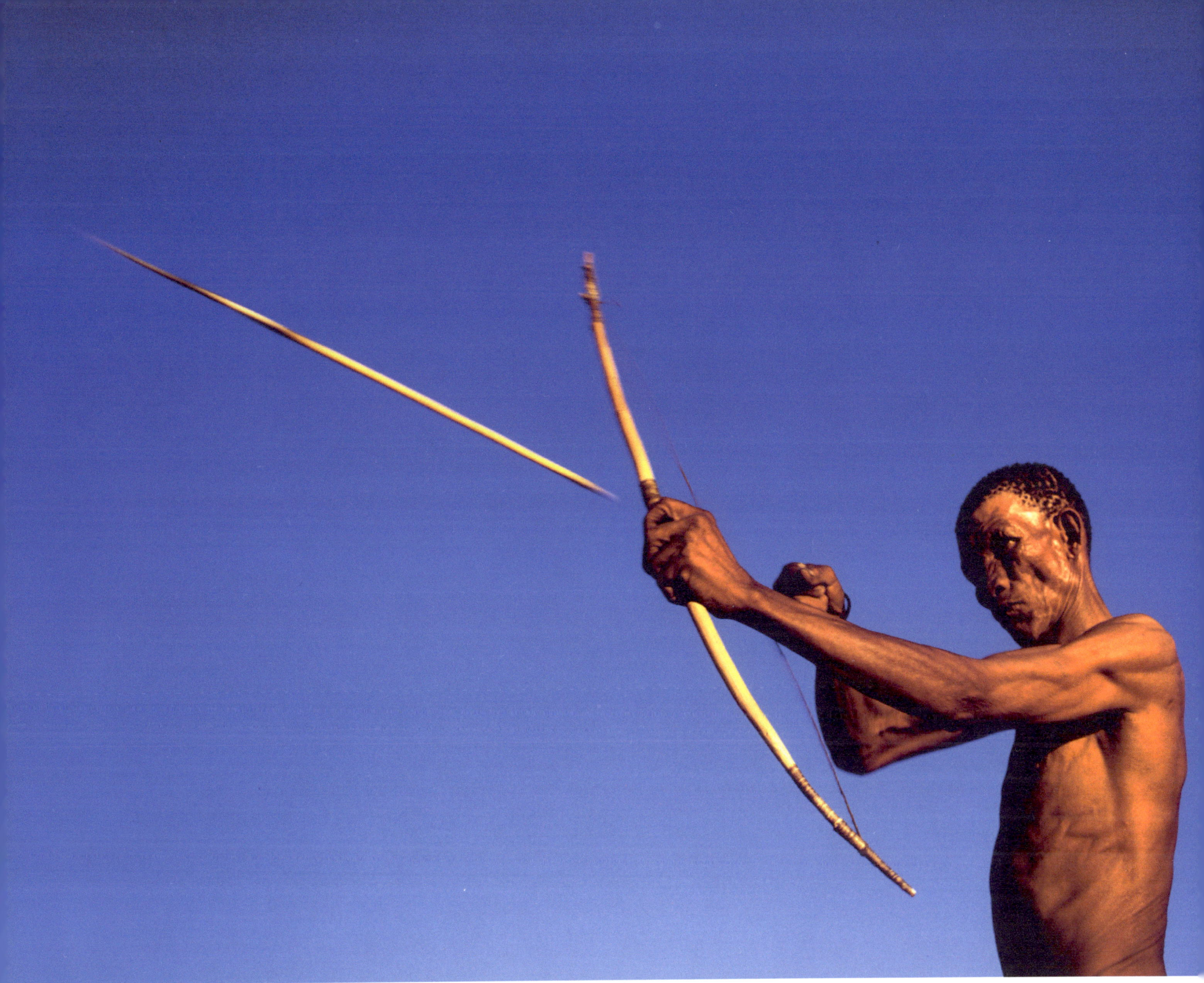

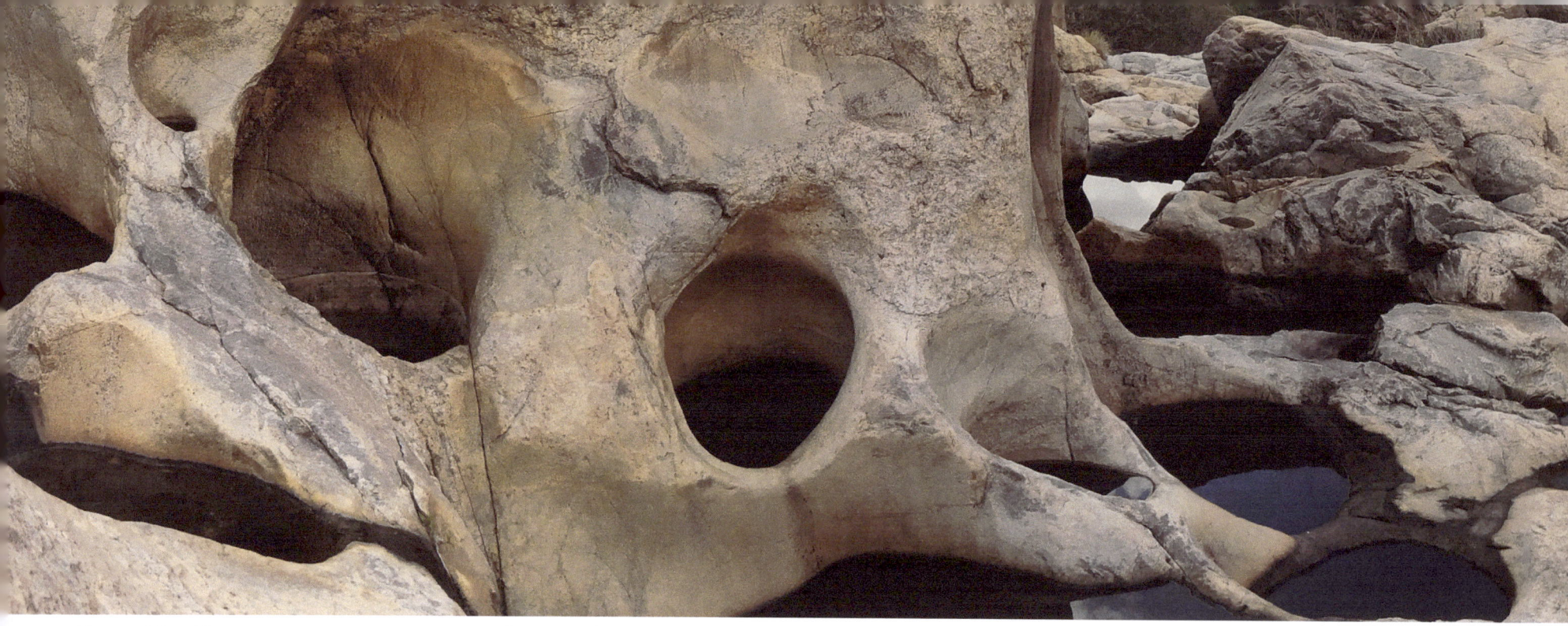

Above: The Komati River near Nsangwini. Places with unusual geology often became sacred sites.

WHAT'S IN A NAME?

For long periods, the San were known as Bushmen or 'Bushman', and sometimes still are. Some San self-identify as Bushmen today. The name 'San' entered academic literature as a replacement to 'Bushmen' to avoid negative connotations from past racist and condescending descriptions. San was borrowed by academics from Nama, a Namibian pastoralist language.

After several years, it became evident that in the Nama language San had negative connotations - meaning 'vagrant' or 'itinerant wanderer'. This created a problem for academics who, with the best of intentions, had replaced one derogatory term with another.

The problem was overcome by pronouncing San as *Saan* - with a long a - and so a new word was created, the negative connotations fell away and academic papers did not have to be altered. Khoisan is a group term that includes Khoe pastoralists from the Cape with the closely related San.

Note: Swaziland changed its name to Eswatini in 2019.

GEOLOGY

Eswatini stretches from the highveld plateau to the lowveld, and has the Lubombo Mountains forming the easern boundary of the country.

The highveld has typical altitudes of 900 to 1400 metres with high rainfall and mist during the summer rainy season. Rivers flow across the country, from west to east, and then cross into Mozambique and flow out into the sea. Heavy highveld rain washes minerals out of the soils, resulting in grasses with low nutritional content. These are unable to support large herds of animals, whether cattle today or herds of antelope in the past.

The lowveld had vast herds of wild animals, though Sleeping Sickness, carried by Tsetse Fly and also malaria, both fatal to humans were common before eradication during the colonial era. The fertile and disease free middleveld was the ecozone of choice by the San for many thousands of years before colonial settlers arrived in Eswatini.

THE POWER REALITY

The San believed that there were two levels of reality. Daily life was clearly visible, but it was interwoven with powerful spirit beings. The spirits had immense power and could affect hunting success, or cause droughts and sickness. The spirits, which often fused human and animal bodies and behaviours, were invisible. This made finding out what they were doing difficult, particularly if there was a serious problem facing the group.

When this happened a trance dance was held. During these events, people would form a circle and shuffle-dance for hours on end. Eventually, there would be a break from ordinary reality and they would enter a trance state. In trance, they believed that they were in the power reality where spirits and beings were visible. They would interact with them and later return to ordinary reality with the solution to the problem. Sometimes what they had seen and experienced was then painted on rock.

STONE TOOLS and HUNTING

Stone tools from the San are found throughout the country, but they are most common in the middleveld. This eco-zone was comparatively disease-free year round, there were large rivers, sufficient animals for hunting, and a wide range of plants that could be gathered for food and medicines.

There was one further geological attraction to the middleveld - unlike the sandy and largely rock-free lowveld - the middleveld had endless large granite boulders. Some of these form natural shelters, overhangs and caves. These shelters were attractive to the San. Many of the shelters contain stone tools and a few have paintings.

The Komati River Valley had a natural combination of factors that made it ideal for San life. Reliable drinking water attracted people and animals, while the many granite boulders along animal trails provided cover for concealment and ambushes when hunting.

Outcrops of fine grained chert, ideal for making stone tools, occurred naturally upstream. Floods carried chert boulders along the riverbed and right across the country, ensuring a constant supply of raw materials for stone tools on the riverbanks.

Right: The Komati River going underground.

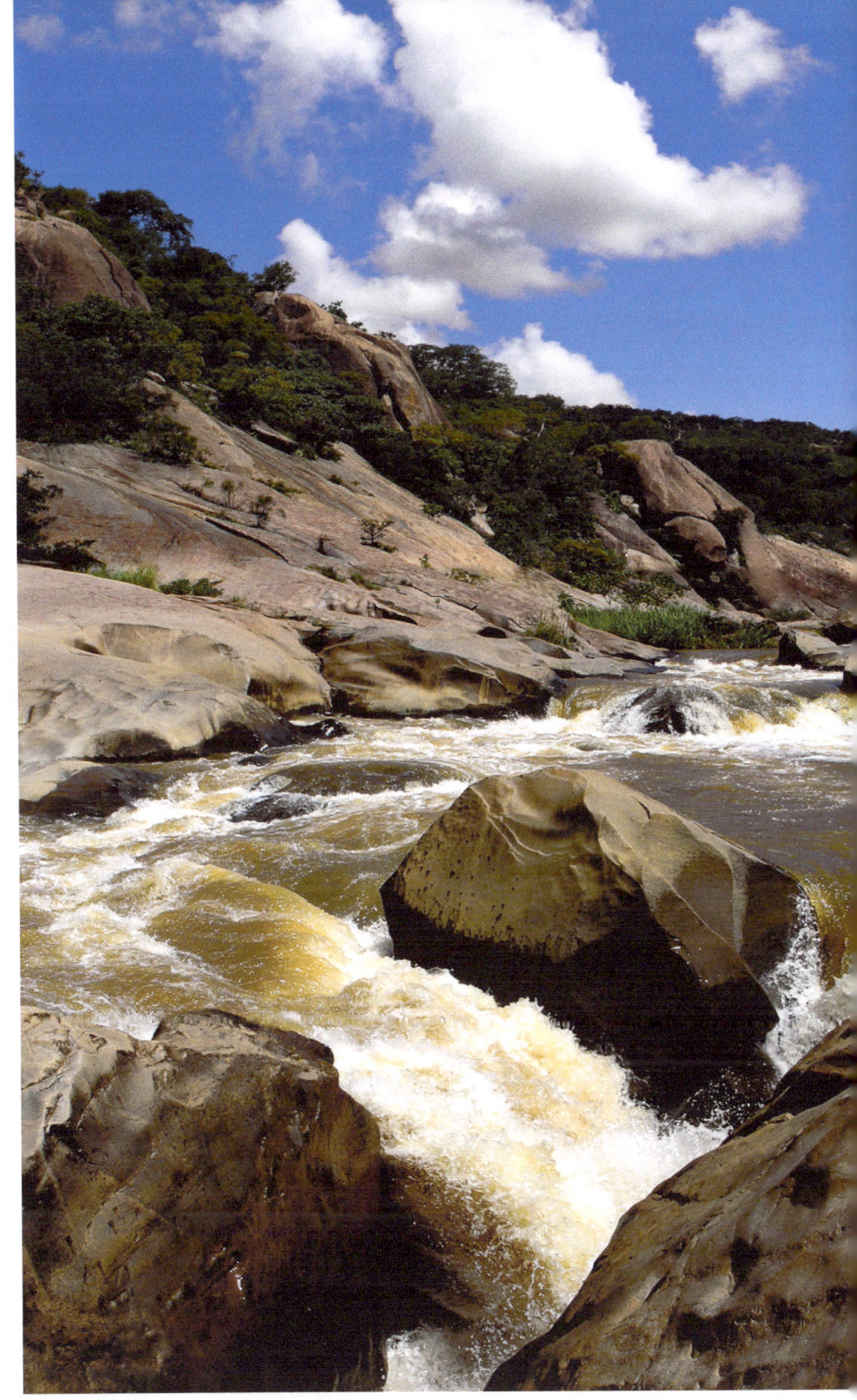

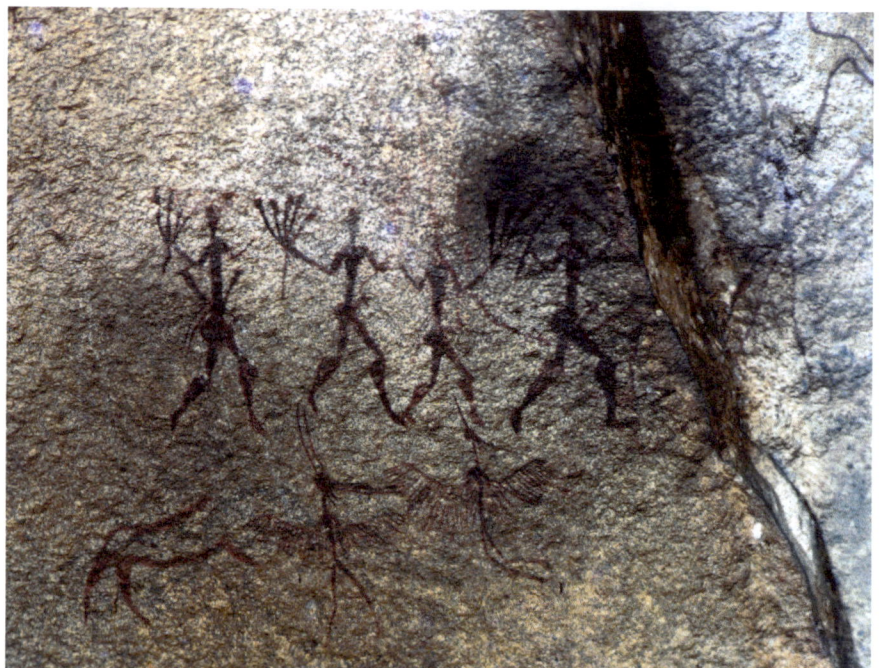

Painting of a trance ceremony at Nsangwini.
Drawing of the scene above.

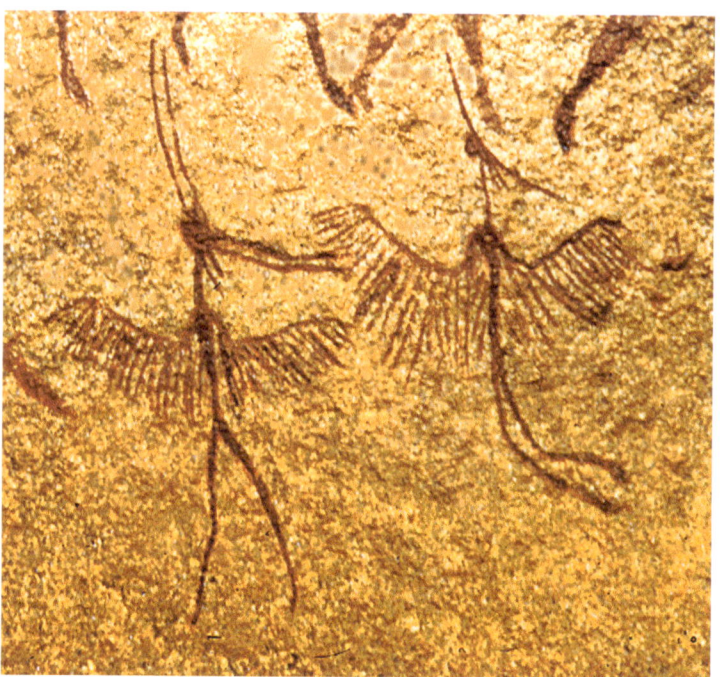

Detail of the flying 'birdmen' from the painting on the left.

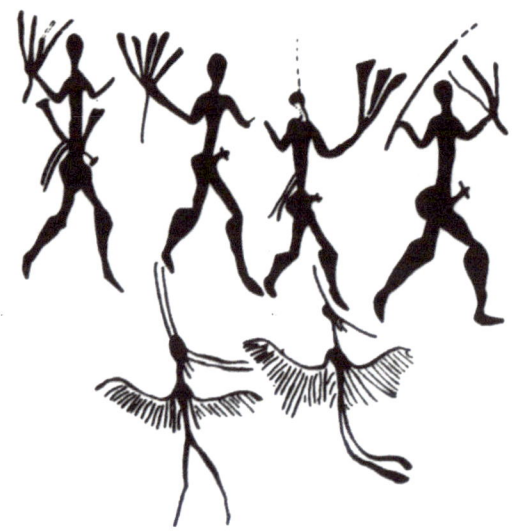

ROCK ART

There are fifty four recorded rock art sites in Eswatini, but six are either blurred or have been destroyed. Most were painted directly onto rock in granite overhangs and shelters. A few are crisp and clear, but most are faded by time.

The paintings on this page are from Nsangwini, a rock shelter overlooking the Komati River. The photo at top left depicts a circular trance dance. Probably the men at the top are carrying branches with stone spear and arrow heads attached to them. Potent energy released during the ceremony would have washed over the spear and arrowheads and remained in them afterwards, improving hunting success. The figures are heading towards a crack in the rock which provided entrance to the power reality.

The two figures at the bottom have entered into the power reality. They have been transformed into beings which fuse praying mantis heads, bird's wings and human bodies. Their bent legs indicate that they are flying.

Directions to Nsangwini are on page 44.

8

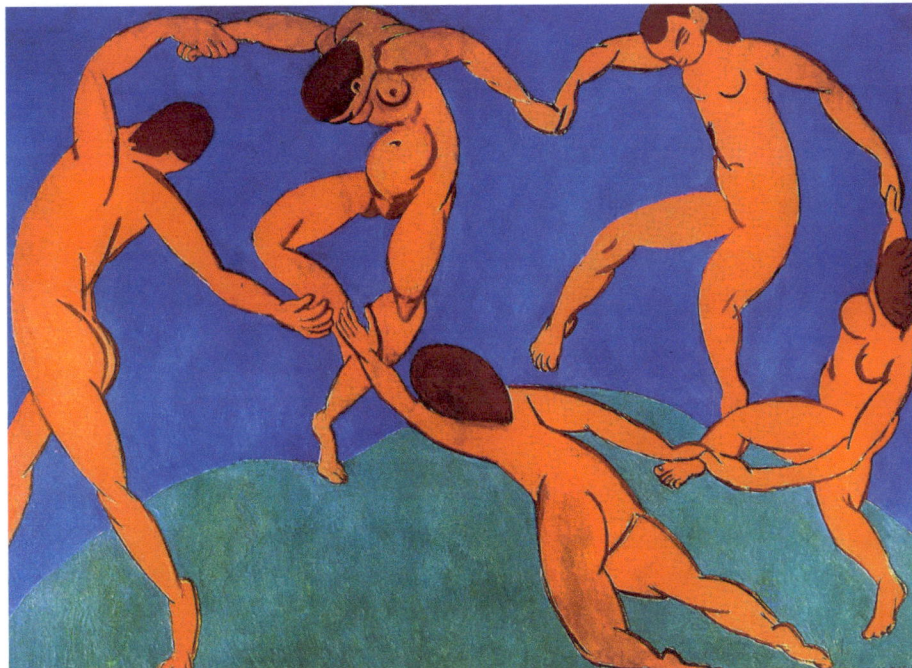

Above: La Danse, Henri Matisse
Right: Circular trance dance

TRANCE DANCES

These were ritual dances that helped the San enter trance states in which they entered the power reality where the spirit beings lived. Trance ceremonies were held to resolve pressing issues such as illness, drought, scarcity of animals or social conflict.

Circular dances were sometimes held in the open, as well as in rock shelters. Painted figures on the walls from previous ceremonies would have flickered in the firelight and appeared to move, enhancing the event.

The painting above by Matisse, *La Danse*, shows how a modern artist depicted a circular three dimensional event in two dimensions without western perspective. This was the same challenge that faced San painters, and they came up with a similar solution in the painting on the right. It depicts a circular trance ceremony.

It is likely that many San paintings are depictions of dances, transformations and power figures from the power reality. These would probably have been painted afterwards for the people who had not entered trance states.

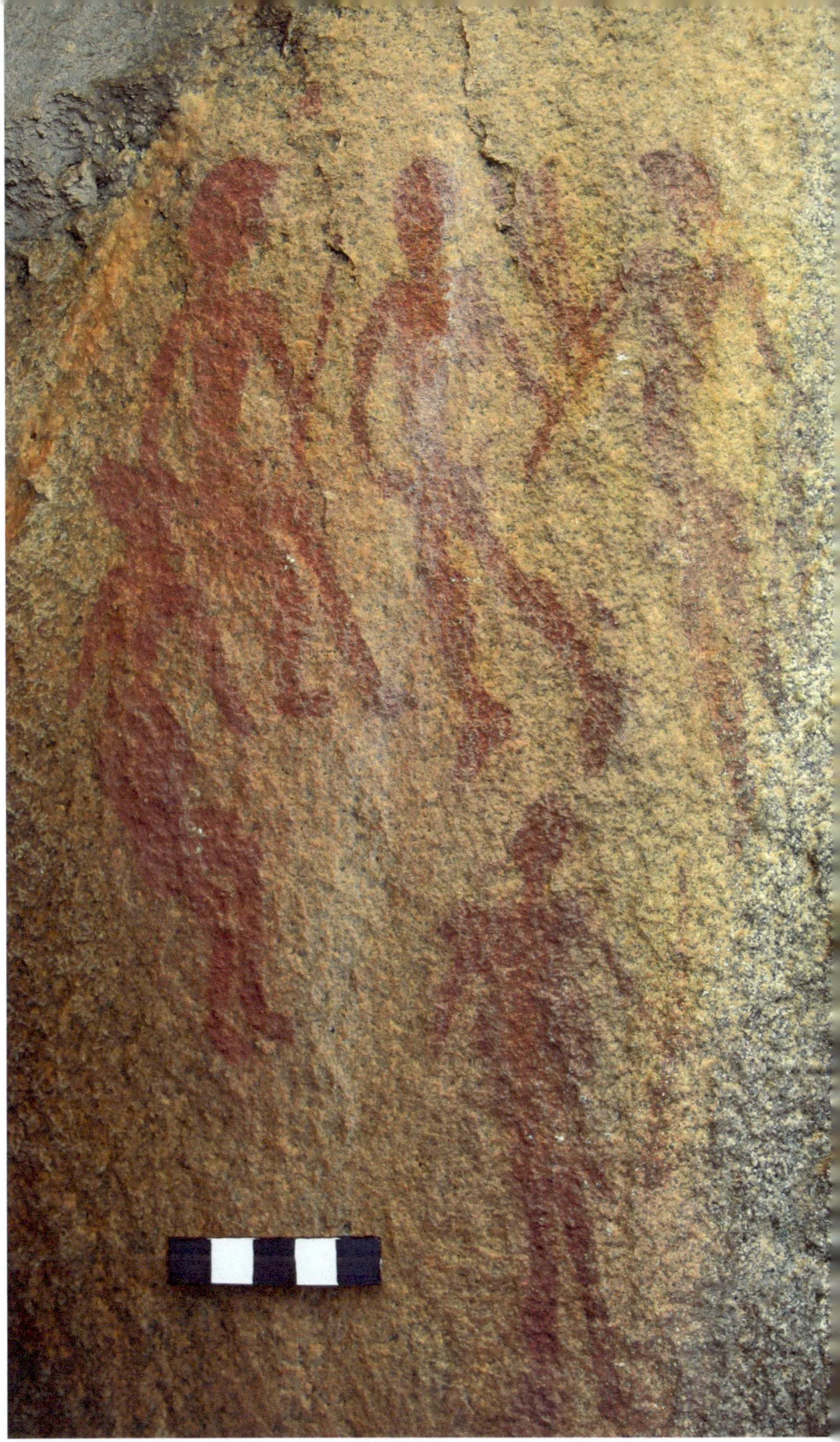

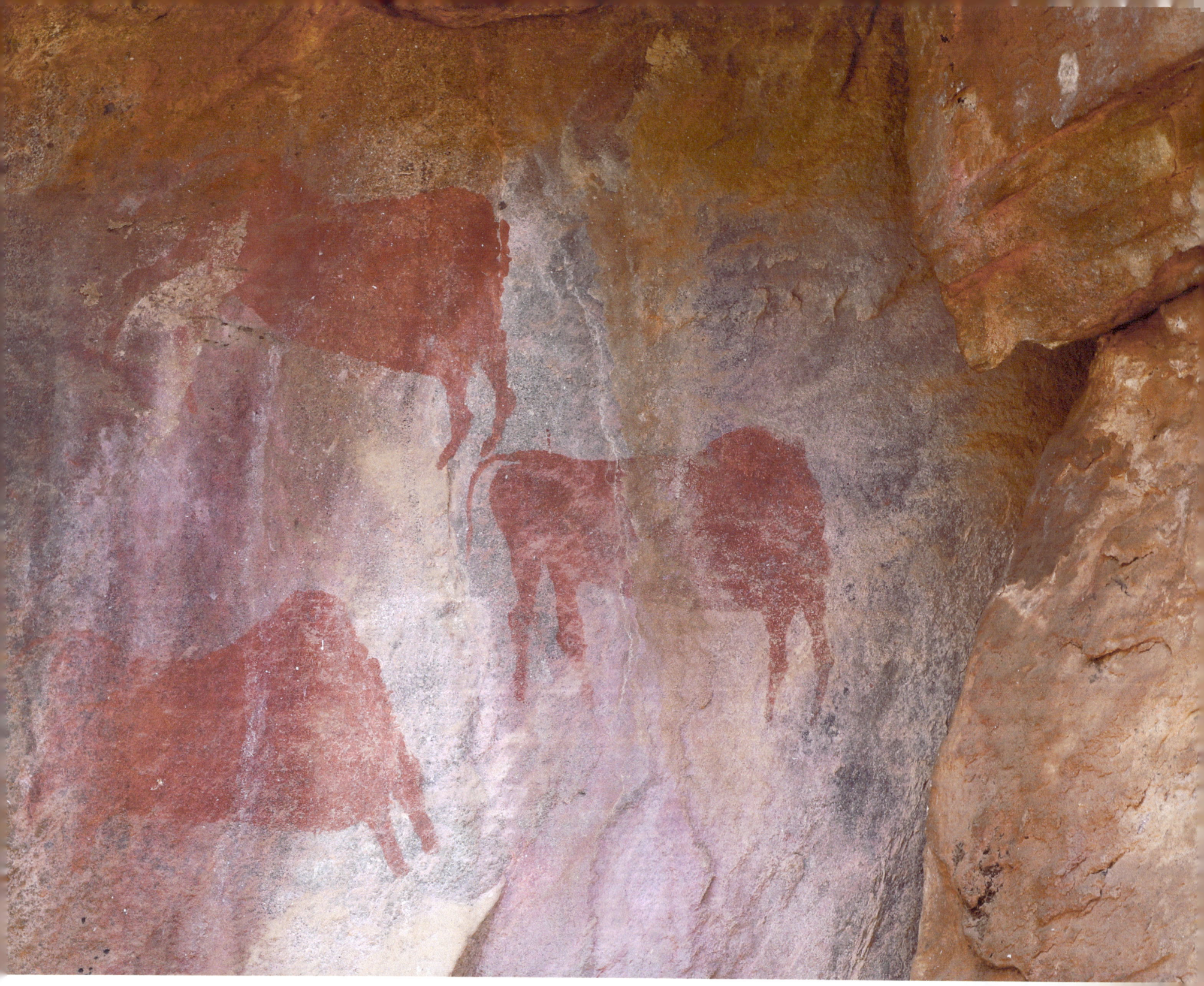

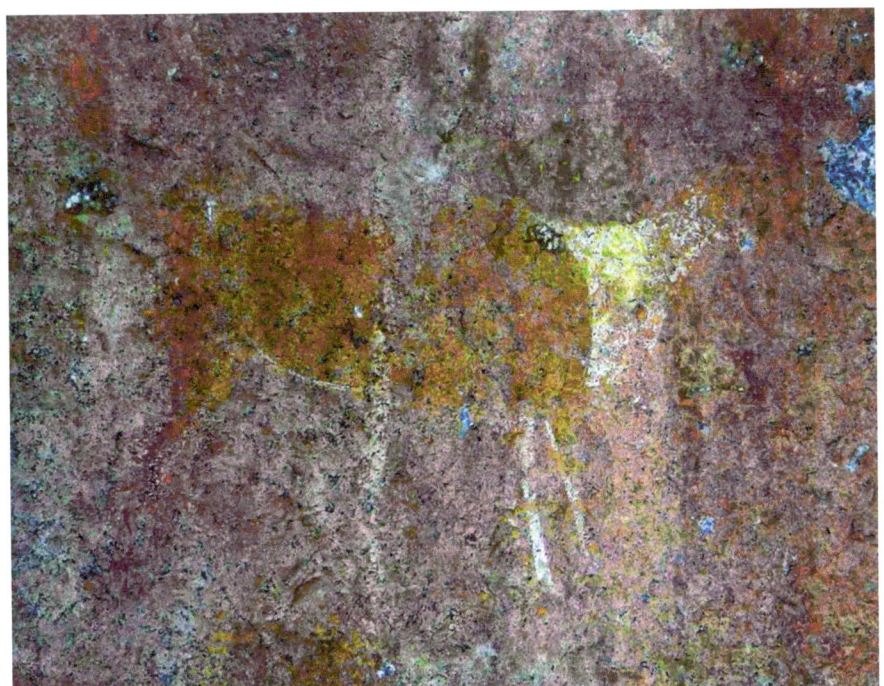

Eland with white head remaining.
Left: Three eland painted on sandstone.

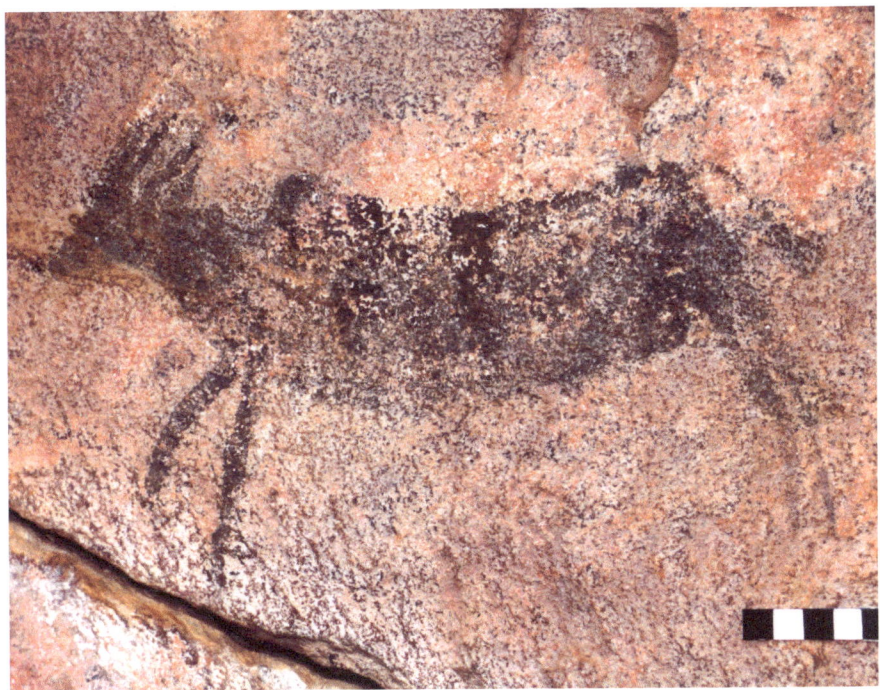

Antelope painted with charcoal.

FERTILITY and ABUNDANCE

Eland are by far the largest antelope in southern Africa. These graceful animals symbolised all that was positive and benevolent in the world to the San. Worldwide hunter-gatherers frequently choose one animal that symbolises and guards their group. For the San along the Drakensberg Escarpment - which includes the Eswatini highveld - it was the eland.

In Eswatini rock art eland are usually painted in threes, the specific beliefs behind the Eland Trinity has been lost. However, the power associated with the paintings has not, and the cultural tradition of paintings as places of power continues. Zionists, who fuse Christian and traditional beliefs, regularly hold circular trance dances directly beneath the paintings on the left.

PAINT

The San painted their trance induced power reality experiences with the most powerful paint possible - ochre mixed with blood, ideally from an eland. Both blood and ochre are extremely iron rich. Oxidised iron or rust is chemically stable. Paints were probably applied using brushes with animal hair tips and hollow porcupine quills which held paint.

White was obtained by mining kaolin, a white clay, and calcium carbonate. Possibly barium (barytes) was also used. This was mixed with binders like egg white or tree sap. The binders were organic and unstable, so the white components of paintings have frequently weathered, leaving the ochre based red paint behind. The white heads of the eland opposite have almost completely weathered away, but some vestiges of white remain. Black was created from manganese, this produced a deep, sometimes purplish black.

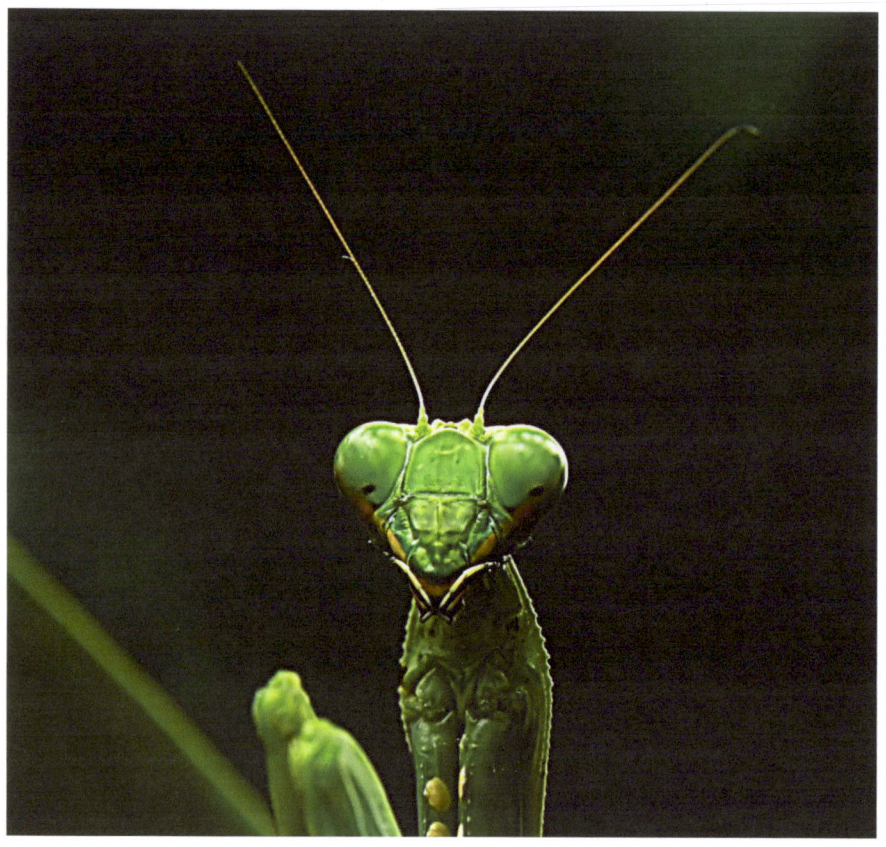

CREATION

To the San !Kaggen was a praying mantis creator/trickster who could shape shift into any animal. Usually, he shifted into eland bulls, snakes or caterpillars. When humans entered trance they too could shape shift, becoming a wide range of animals. These photos show people who have partially shifted into mantis during trance. Their bodies are painted with horizontal stripes of red and white ochre, and on their backs there are either small mantis wings or fly whisks. Fly whisks were carried during trance to absorb power for ritual use afterwards to clear negativity.

Top: Praying mantis.
Right: DStretch enhanced mantis figure, with increased detail.
Far right: Painting of human/mantis figures during a trance ceremony.

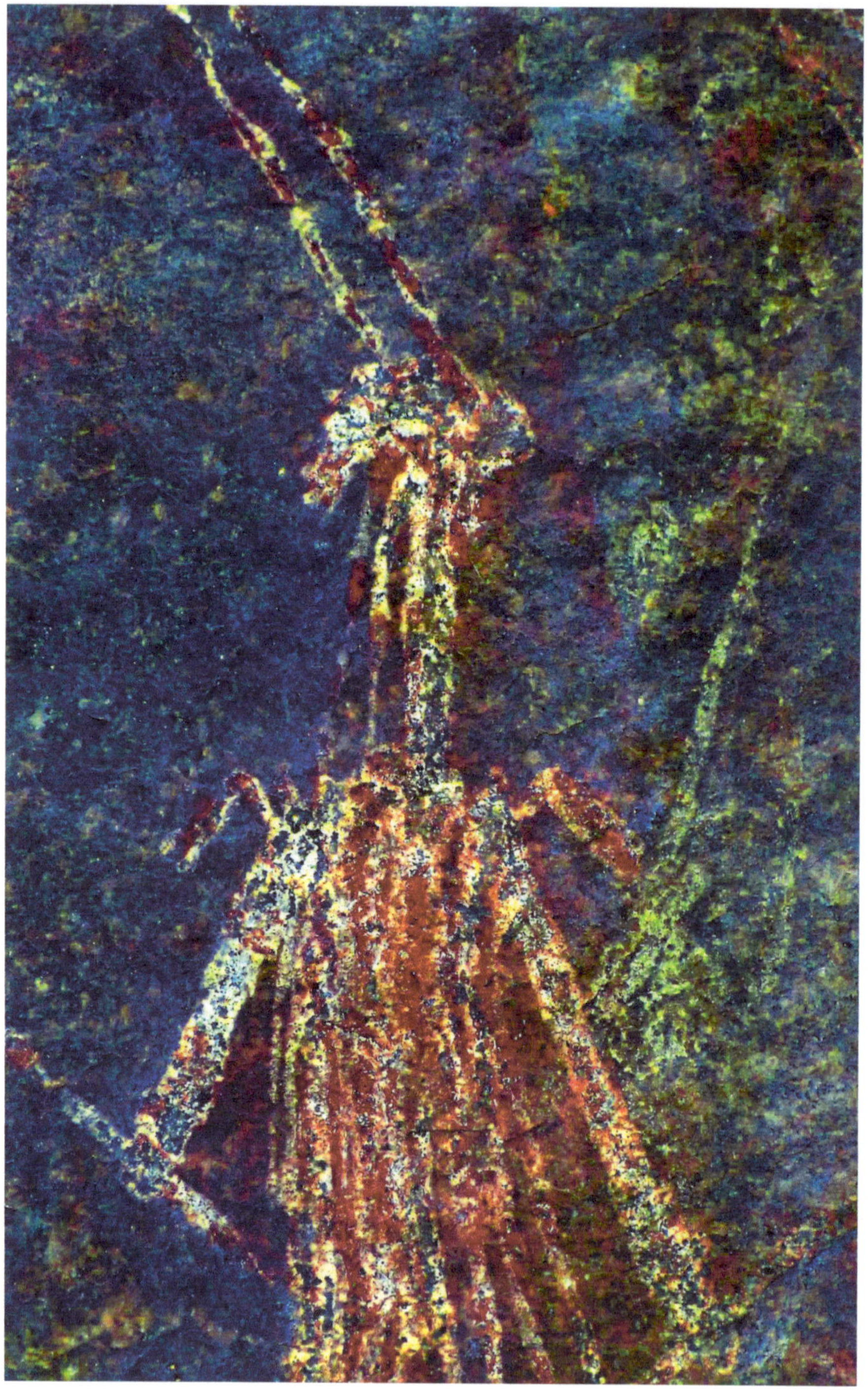

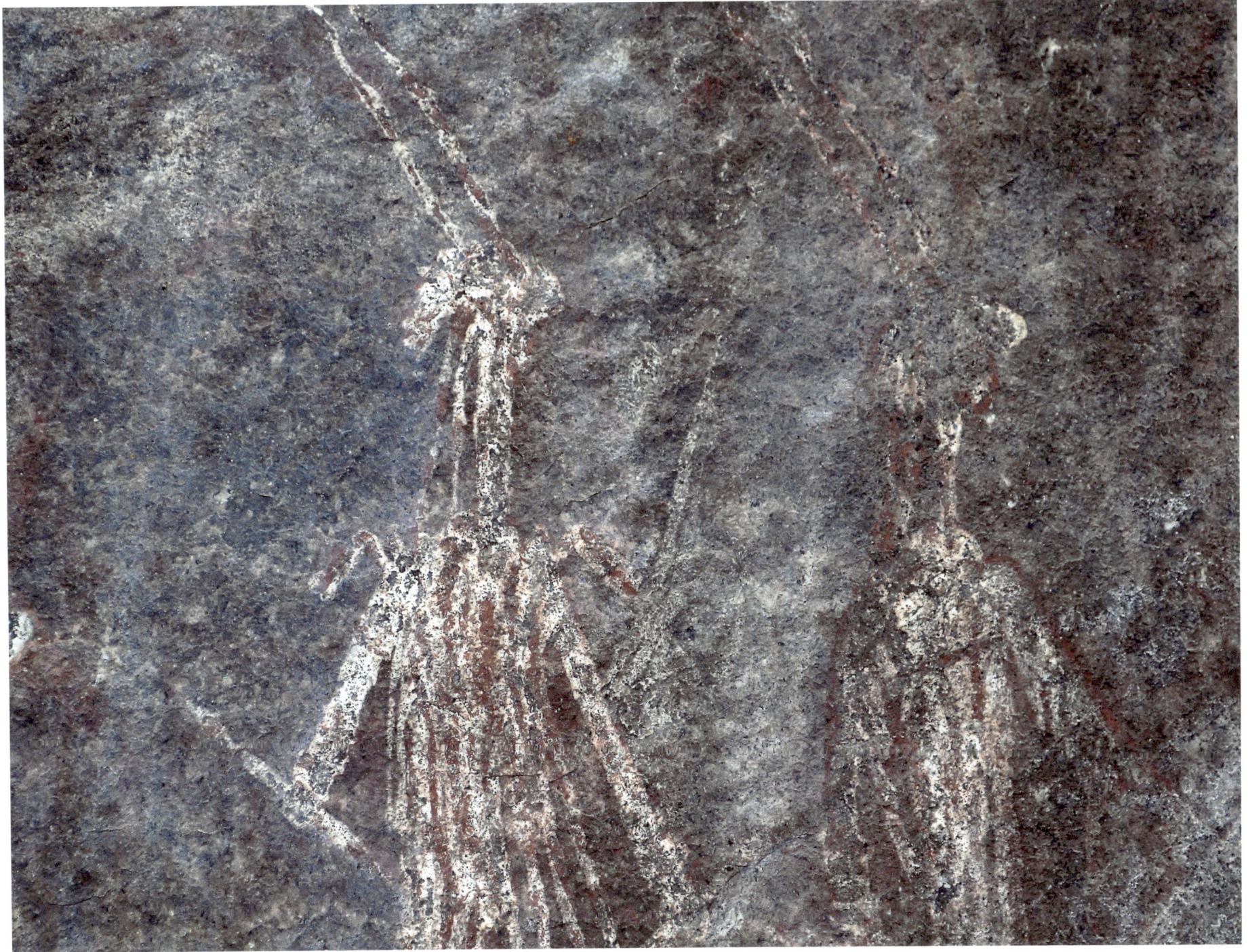

WHAT DO PAINTINGS MEAN?

The San power reality was interwoven with every aspect of daily life. There was no hard boundary between ordinary reality and the power reality. Power beings that combined human and animal bodies and abilities - known as therianthropes - were encountered in the power reality during trance and in dreams. The resulting fusion of senses and abilities made them far more powerful than either humans or animals on their own. By finding out what therianthropes were doing one could resolve issues in daily life. Whilst this explains why people entered trance, and why so many therianthropes were painted, it does not provide detail.

Fortunately, a German linguist and a relative collected thousands of pages of San beliefs in the late 1800s from San who did paint. There are also a few recorded early colonial contacts with San painters. When combined, these sometimes allow researchers to match specific beliefs to paintings. Although based on ethnography, the resulting analyses are often vigorously debated in academic journals.

Some paintings were individualistic, reflecting what artists saw and experienced. There were regional belief cults too, like the winged birdmen of the Komati, which were limited to a small area. We can plot their distribution, but will probably never uncover their subtle meanings.

Other subjects were widespread. Eland were central to San cosmology, providing powerful positive energy when alive, and releasing potent energy when they died. As a result they were frequently painted. Eland fat was a powerful strengthener that could be carried around and applied when needed. Ochre was a connector that helped lift the veil of the power reality so that people could see the true causes of events, and remedy them.

Some San beliefs have parallels worldwide. Powerful flying therianthropes with human bodies and bird's wings are more familiar today as angels. An ordinary reality dominated by a power reality - inhabited by invisible beings with awesome super-human abilities - lies at the core of Judaism, Christianity and Islam.

Right: The full praying mantis painting, showing painted dancing figures.

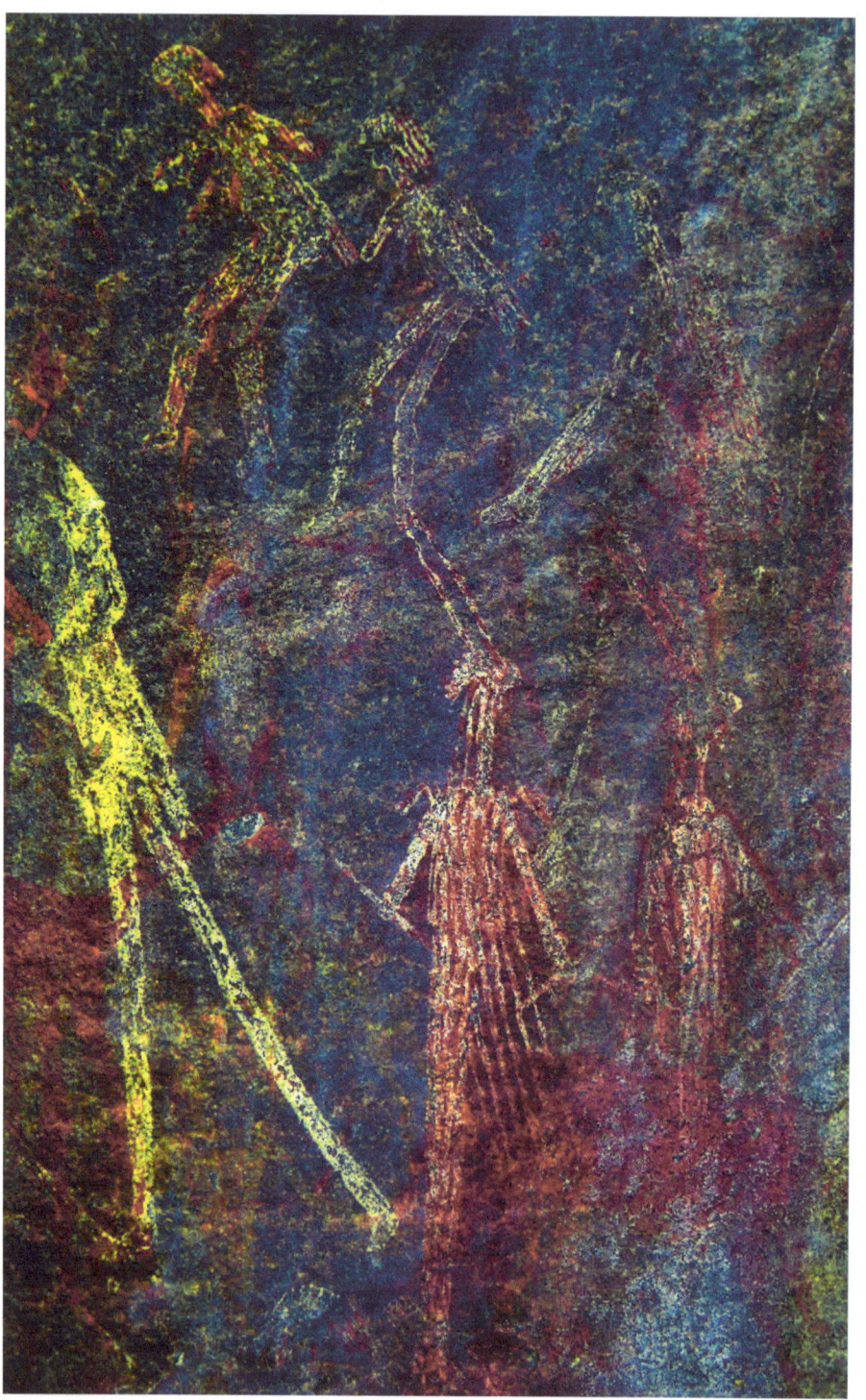

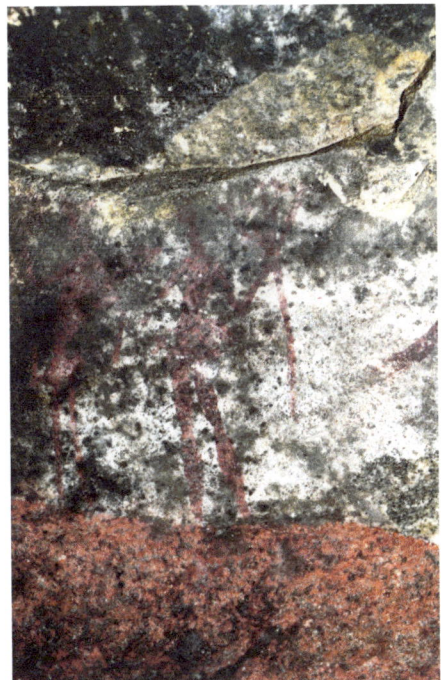 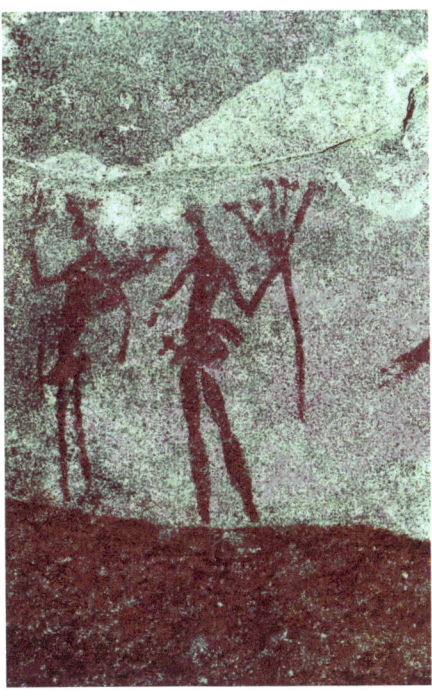 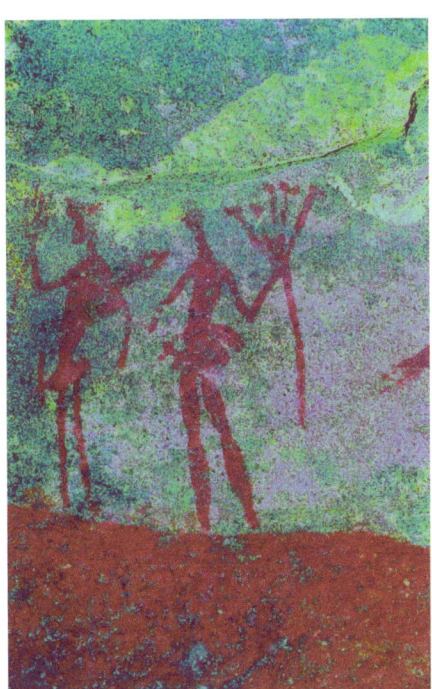 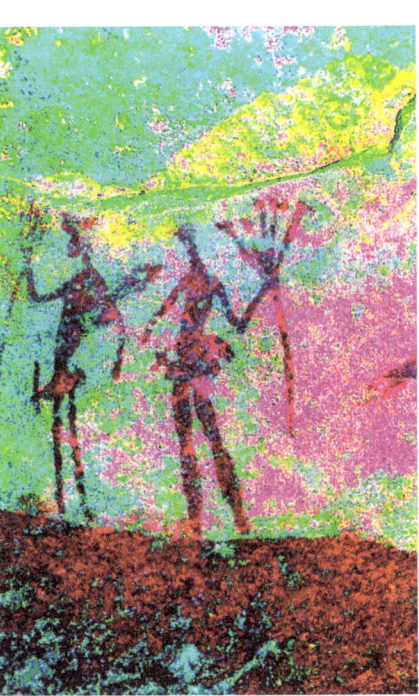

A section of rock painting on the left with three variations in different colour wavelengths.

ENHANCING ROCK ART

Interpreting rock art within its cultural context is complex. But there is another challenge - the ability to actually see what was painted.

High resolution digital cameras record minute detail that our eyes simply do not see. When this facility is combined with the enhancement of specific wavelengths, whole features that are not apparent to the naked eye become obvious.

DStretch is an app for phone and computer that is specifically designed to enhance faded rock art. Different colour combinations can provide detail that is often invisible to the naked eye. Compare the row of photos above.

The original photo is on the left and is barely distinguishable. Three successive differing colour combinations reveal new features. Taken as a total, what was a reddish brown blur emerges as two clear male figures holding spear-points attached to branches during a trance ceremony.

WHY ROCK PAINTINGS DECAY

There are ninety two naturally occurring stable elements on this planet. Ochre is iron oxide - rust - and does not break down into anything else, it has reached it's stable state. So, once painted on rock, ochre could last indefinitely, yet rock paintings decay.

There are several reasons for this. Granite appears immensely solid, but is porous, allowing water to slowly seep through it. When water in the rock eventually reaches the surface it carries dissolved salts with it. When the water evaporates, the salts crystallise behind painted surfaces, slowly flaking the paint off. Water also washes down some painted surfaces, taking the ochre with it. Fungus grows in damp places and sometimes covers paintings, destroying them. Heating and cooling cracks granite, plates of rock drop off, taking paintings with them.

In southern Eswatini, people sometimes painted on smooth, flat sandstone. This tends to weather fast, disintegrating into fine sand, along with any paintings.

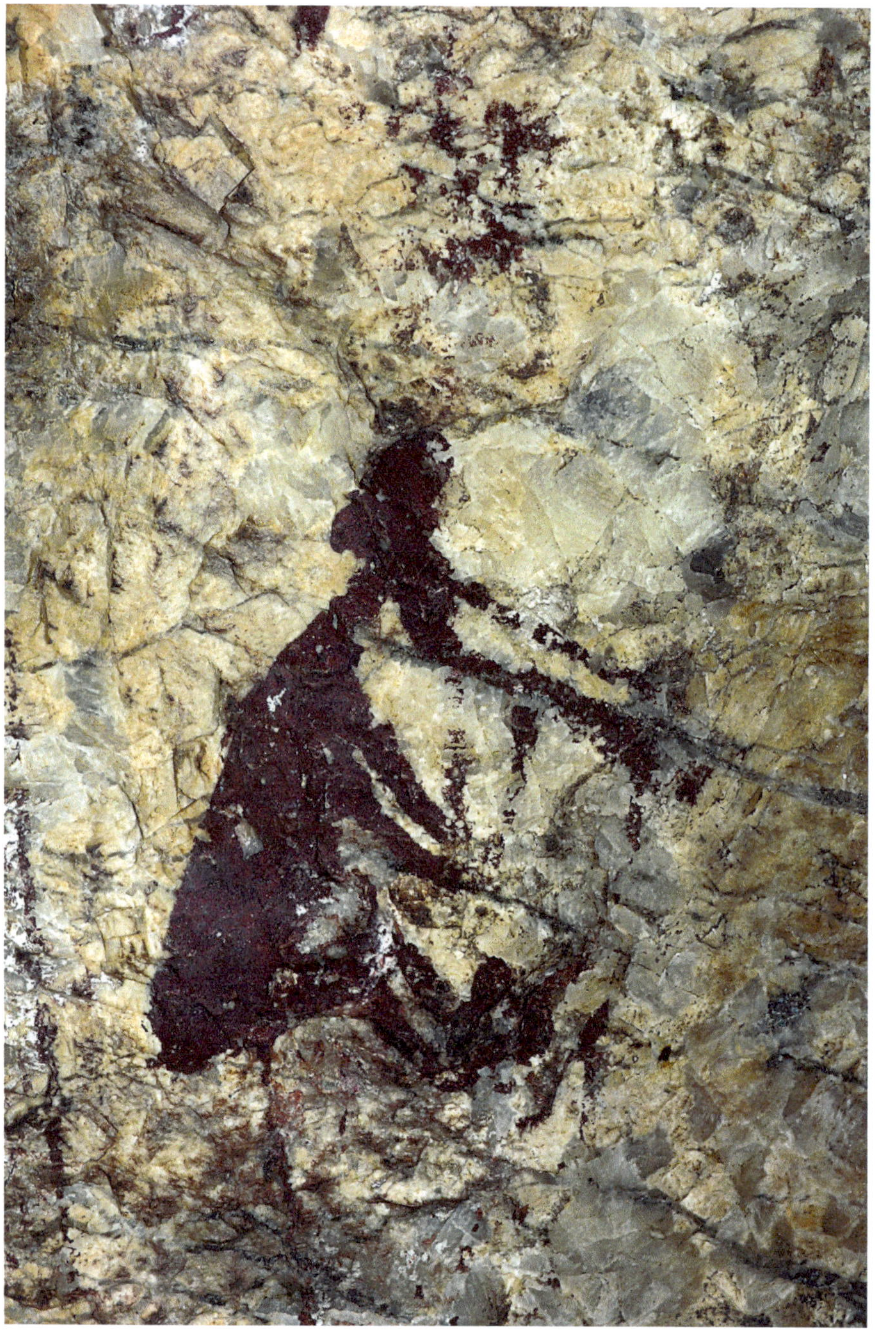

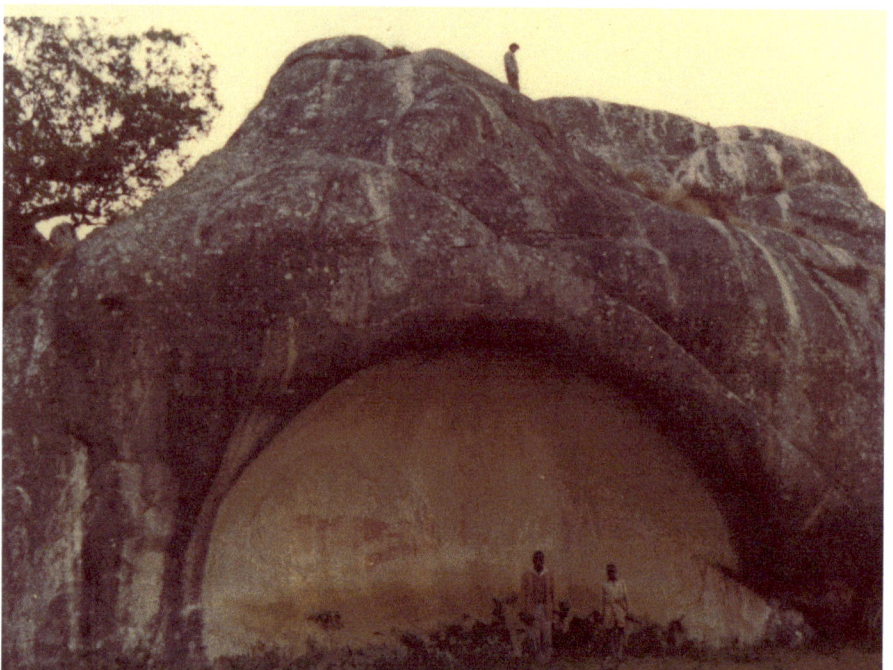

MUSIC and HALLUCINATIONS

People often used drums to enhance the trance experience. The painting on the left is of a drummer. The preferred sites for trance ceremonies were granite rock shelters which naturally amplified sound. The San believed that the power reality lay behind rock faces. This could have originated because it seems as though sound is coming through the rock.

Worldwide, people see similar shapes in trance, often these are zig-zags, shimmering lines and other geometric patterns. People probably painted these patterns onto their bodies in preparation for trance experiences.

The painting on the right, of a man's legs, show zig-zags in red ochre and white paint. The painting is faded from weathering - above it a DStretch image shows the geometric patterns more clearly in false colour.

The photos on the far right were taken in the Komati Valley in the early 21st century. They show the wall decorations in a *sangoma's* bedroom and also their *mdumba*, or consulting room. Like the San, many healers in Eswatini enter trance as part of their healing practice.

Above: Painting of a drummer during a ritual ceremony.
Right: A naturally occurring rock formation which amplifies sound.

16

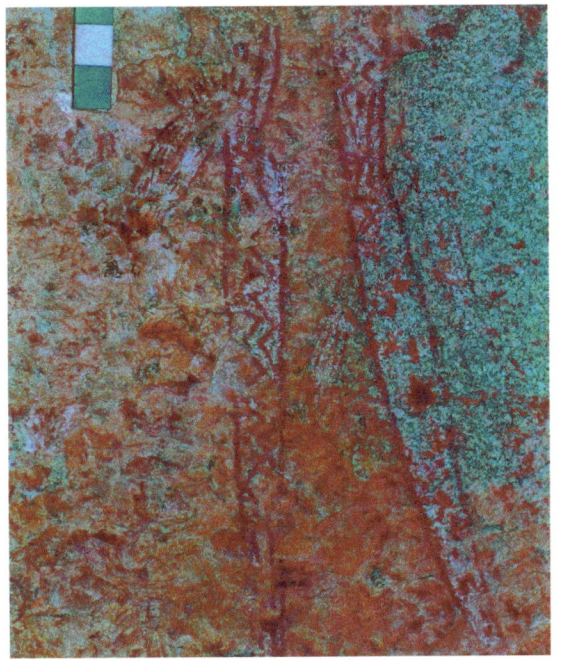

DStretch enhanced image from below.

San legs with geometric patterns.

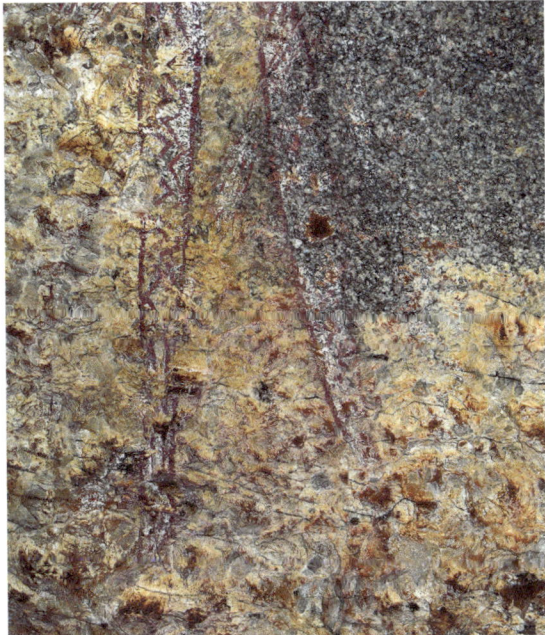

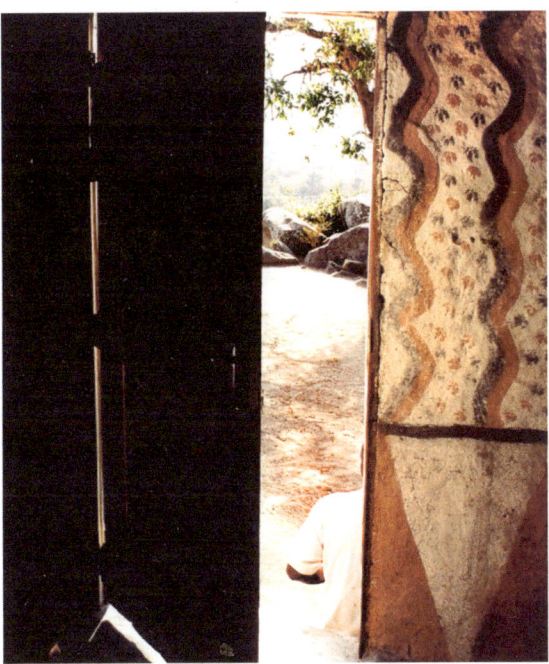

Patterns in a sangoma's bedroom, Komati.

A sangoma's consulting room, Komati.

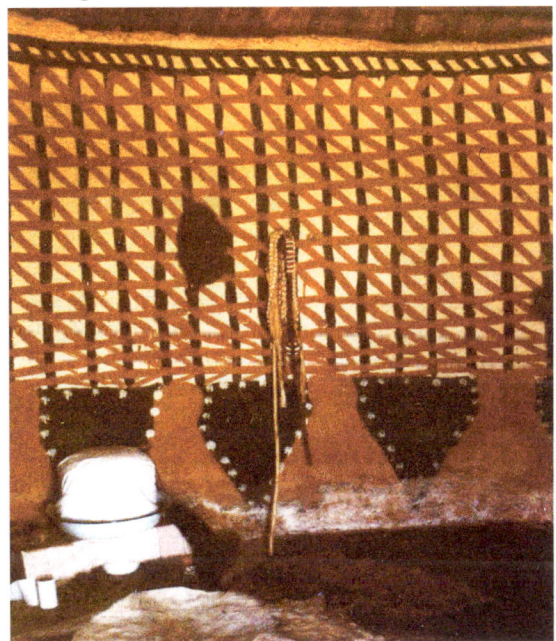

WHAT DID THE SAN PAINT?

Most San paintings in Eswatini are believed to be depictions of encounters in the power reality. The paintings do not appear to have been part of a large composition before starting, like most western art. Instead they were simply added wherever there was a suitable surface, sometimes fresh paintings were completed over older faded paintings. The result is a complex mixture that could have been painted over thousands of years.

There are, however, three sites in the country with a clear aesthetic intent by the artist. One of them, of a feline, is opposite. The other two are a composition of three eland bulls and a group of rhebuck. They are on pages 10 and 21.

The feline on the right was painted on rough granite. Because of the uneven rock surface, the artist prepared a smooth surface made from thick white paste to paint on. This surface preparation is believed to be unique in southern Africa. It is identified as a feline because the cat species cannot be determined - it could be a cheetah, a leopard or even a lioness.

The table below gives the frequency of species from 48 surveyed sites in the country.

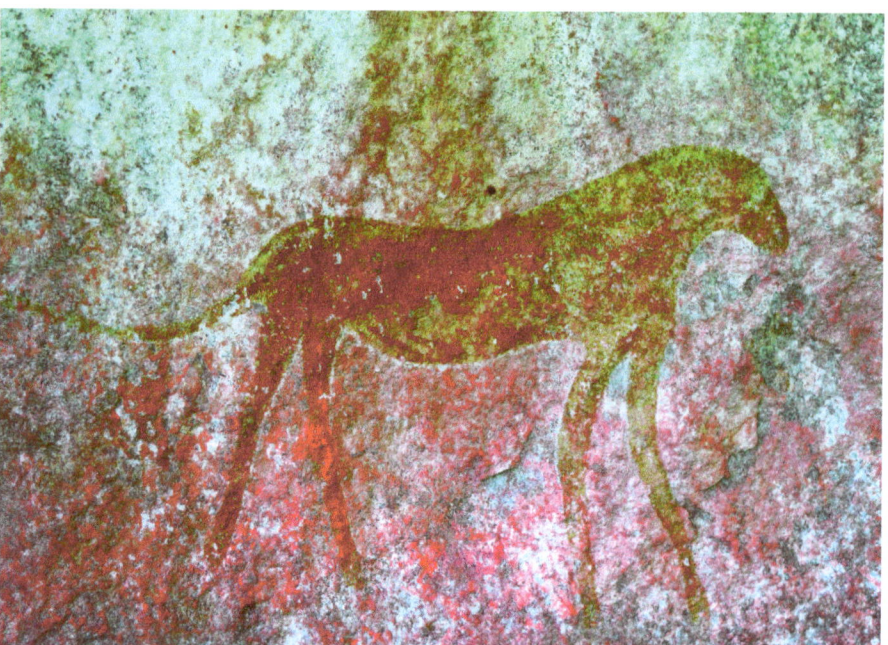

Above: DStretch image of a feline on the facing page.
Right: Finely painted composition of a feline.

PAINTING STATISTICS

Sites with one colour	(including unidentified animal/figure)	33	68,7%
Sites with two colours	(including unidentified animal/figure)	5	10,4%
Sites with three colours	(including unidentified animal/figure)	8	16,6%
Sites with four colours	(including unidentified animal/figure)	1	2,1%
Sites with five colours	(including unidentified animal/figure)	1	2,1%
TOTAL FIGURES	597		

Red monochrome	470	78,8%
Black monochrome	17	2,8%
Orange monochrome	26	4,4%
Brown monochrome	16	2,7%
White monochrome	9	1,5%
Yellow monochrome	17	2,8%
Bichrome figures	42	7,0%

Site - most figures - Nsangwini	160	
Sites - one figure only (inc. unidentified)	6	12,5%
Sites - unidentified animals or figures only	1	2,1%
Sites - animals only (inc. unidentified animals/figures	16	33,3%
Sites - humans only (inc. unidentified figures/animals)	4	8,3%
Sites - antelope only (inc. unidentified figures/animals)	12/48	25,0%
Sites - eland only	3	6,2%
TOTAL FIGURES	597	

Average figures per site	12	
Total unidentified animals	54	8,9%
Total unidentified figures	79	13,3%
Total humans	241	40,4%
Total animals	200	33,5%
Total geometrics	10	1,7%
Total antelope	174	29,1%
Total eland	51	8,6%
Total animal/human composites	10	1,7%

Other: elephant 5 (0,8%), giraffe 7 (1,2%), feline 6 (1%), sheep 5 (0,8%), rhebuck 9 (1,5%), wildebeest 6 (1%), rain animals 3 (0,5%) Symbolic 3 (0,5%)

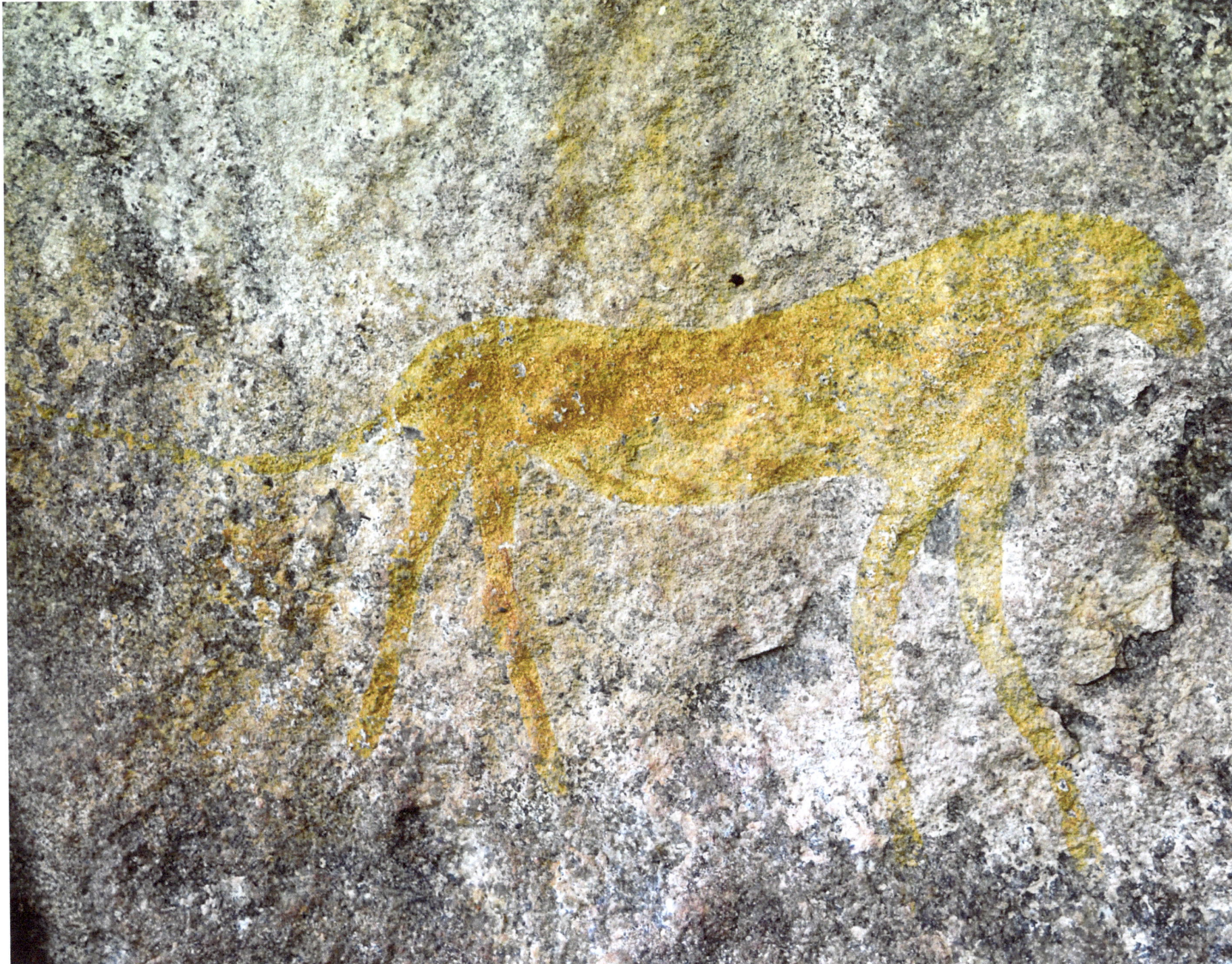

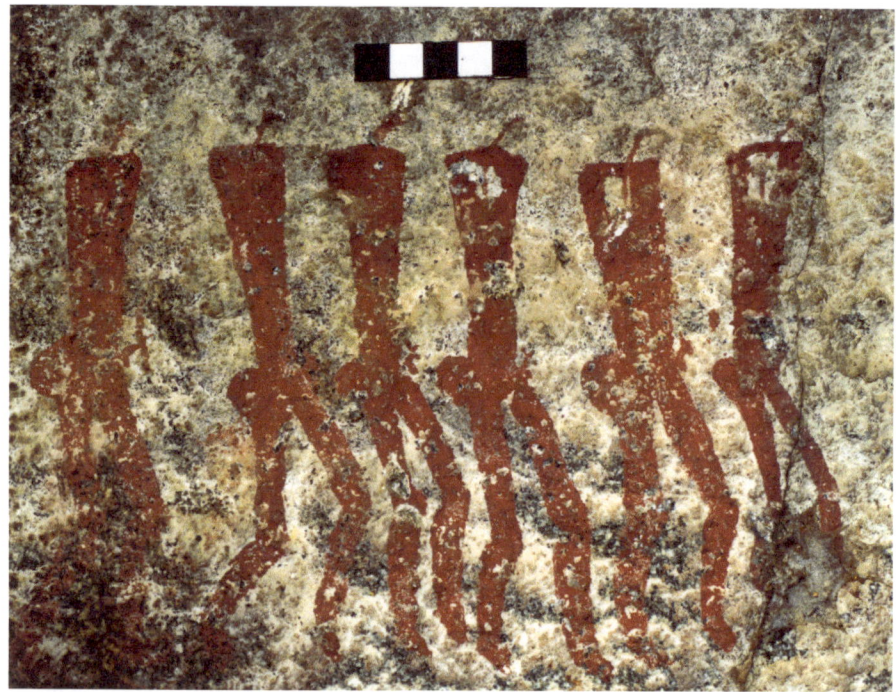

A row of headless dancing men with erections.

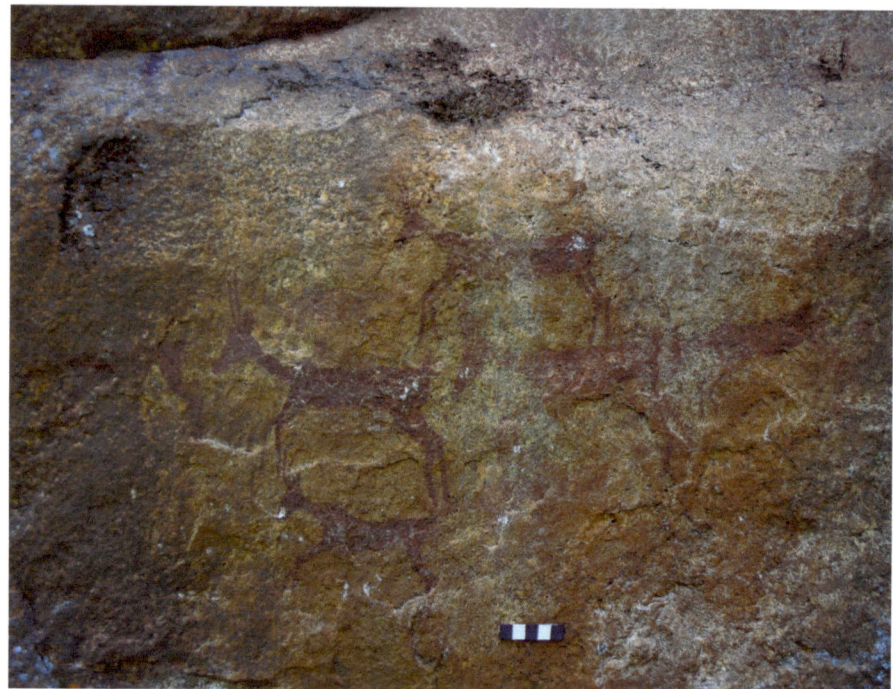

A decorative composition of rhebuck, enhanced image opposite.

LOST WORLDS

Many San paintings depict other realities which can only be understood through their cultural or physical context, something which is often missing or incomplete today.

The painting above shows a row of dancing men. Their heads are missing, presumably because they were painted in unstable white leaving the much longer lasting red ochre behind.

Some San men may have had permanent semi-erect penises, making it difficult to tell if they were sexually aroused or not. All the mens' penises in the painting above have a bar across them, this is likely to have been a penis decoration.

Around half of the paintings of San men in southern Africa have some form of penis decoration. Whether these were clipped on, or were suspended from holes in the foreskin is not known. Some of the penis decorations appear to have been elaborate constructions, with feathers and other light, but decorative components.

DATING ROCK ART

We do not know how old the paintings are. From style, preservation and history, the oldest are probably around 4 000 years old, and the most recent about 170. The older paintings are very similar stylistically to dated paintings in the Drakensberg. These are similar to the headless men (above left), and other single colour red ochre paintings in the book.

Paintings can sometimes be carbon dated, but this is unreliable. Veld fires cause a lot of smoke which is rich in carbon and can contaminate samples taken directly from the paintings.

The most secure way of dating rock art on granite is to excavate the shelter floor below the paintings. Granite exfoliates dish shaped pieces of rock fairly regularly which land beneath the paintings and are then slowly buried. By dating the archaeological layers surrounding the fallen pieces, dates for the paintings can be determined. This has not been attempted in Eswatini, though there are several suitable sites.

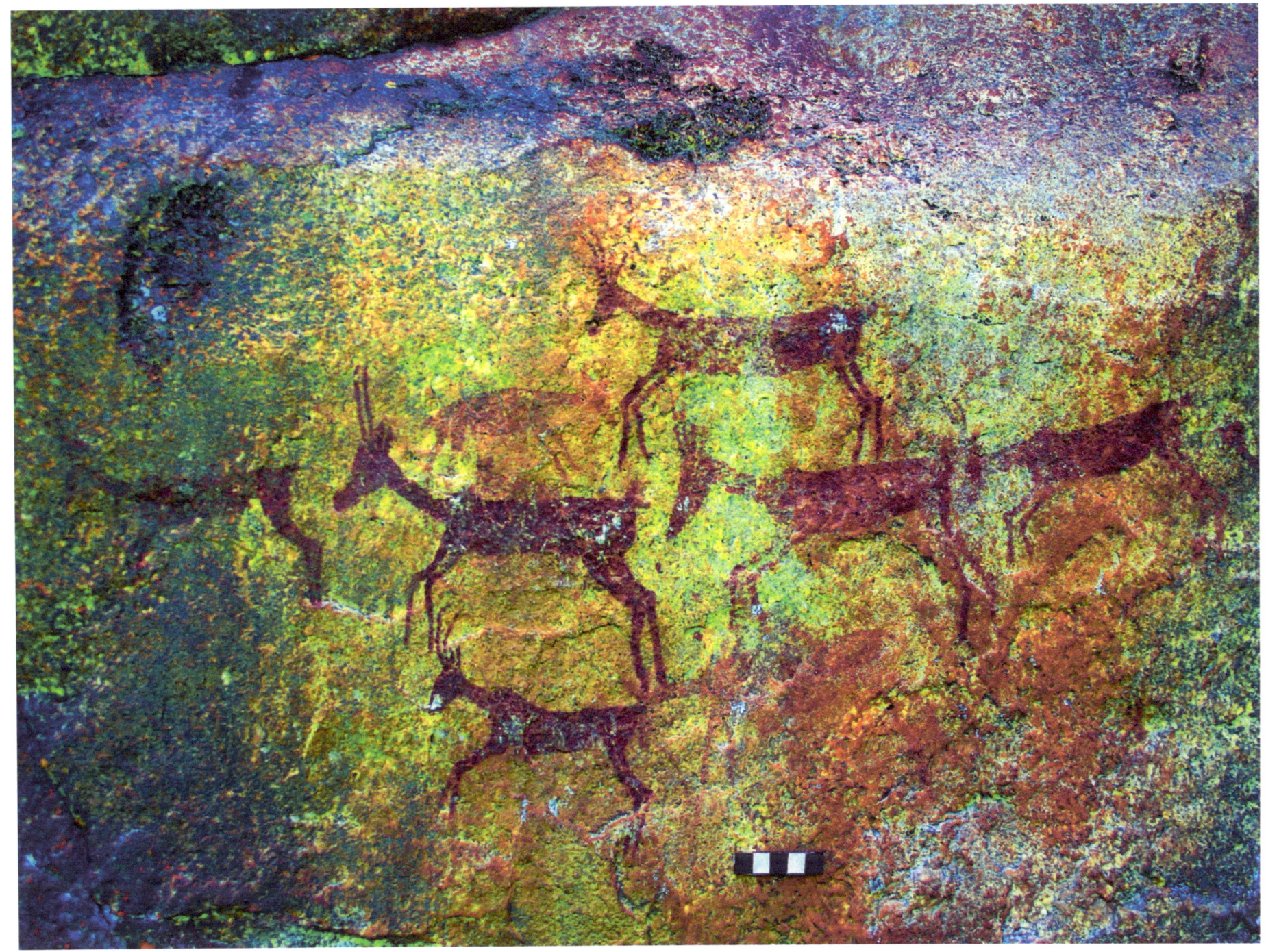

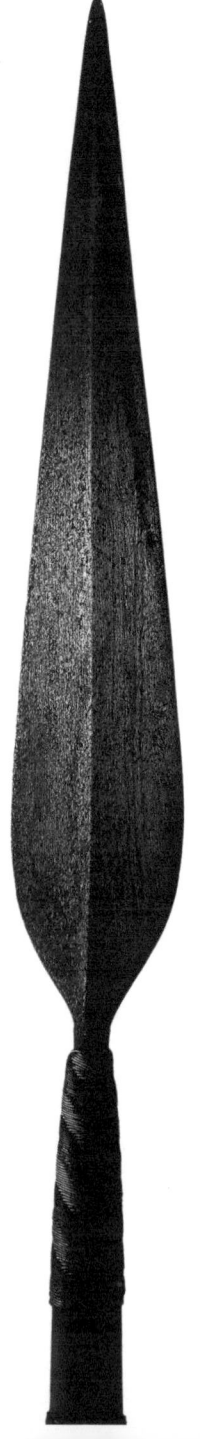

BLACK SETTLERS

For tens of thousands of years, the San and their ancestors before them lived in southern Africa. They hunted and gathered, moving across a vast landscape with few people in it. People took what they needed from the area and moved on, guarded by beings in the power reality. The land was fertile and, because they could move at will and there were few people, serious food shortages would have been comparatively rare. Generation blended into generation; their way of life remained undisturbed for millennia.

Around 400 CE - 1600 years ago - the first black settlers arrived in Eswatini from the north. We do not know what language they spoke, nor where they came from. We do know that they brought an entirely new way of life with them - farming. They arrived with domestic animals, certainly sheep, and possibly cattle too. They also brought new concepts, like the ownership of animals. The San would probably have been amazed at the power and control that the new settlers had over animals. They would also have wondered why they planted crops like millet when there were so many wild plant foods to be had.

The settlers also smelted iron to make spears and hoes for farming. These would have been totally new to people used to making tools from stone.

Hunter-gatherers tend to only own what they can carry, and view animals as common property available to all. Actual ownership of an animal results from hunting and killing it. The San killed animals when they came across them - including the animals that the black farmers had carefully raised and protected.

These different concepts of property caused long running conflicts. But the San had a powerful point on their side. They were accepted as highly skilled rain makers. During periodic droughts the farmers appealed to the San to make the rain return, providing the San with status and a strong bargaining position.

Left: A late iron age Swazi spear from hand forged metal.
Opposite: Black settlers painted at Nsangwini with fat tailed sheep and cattle. The date of the painting is unknown, but it is not more than 1600 years old, the period when the first black settlers arrived.

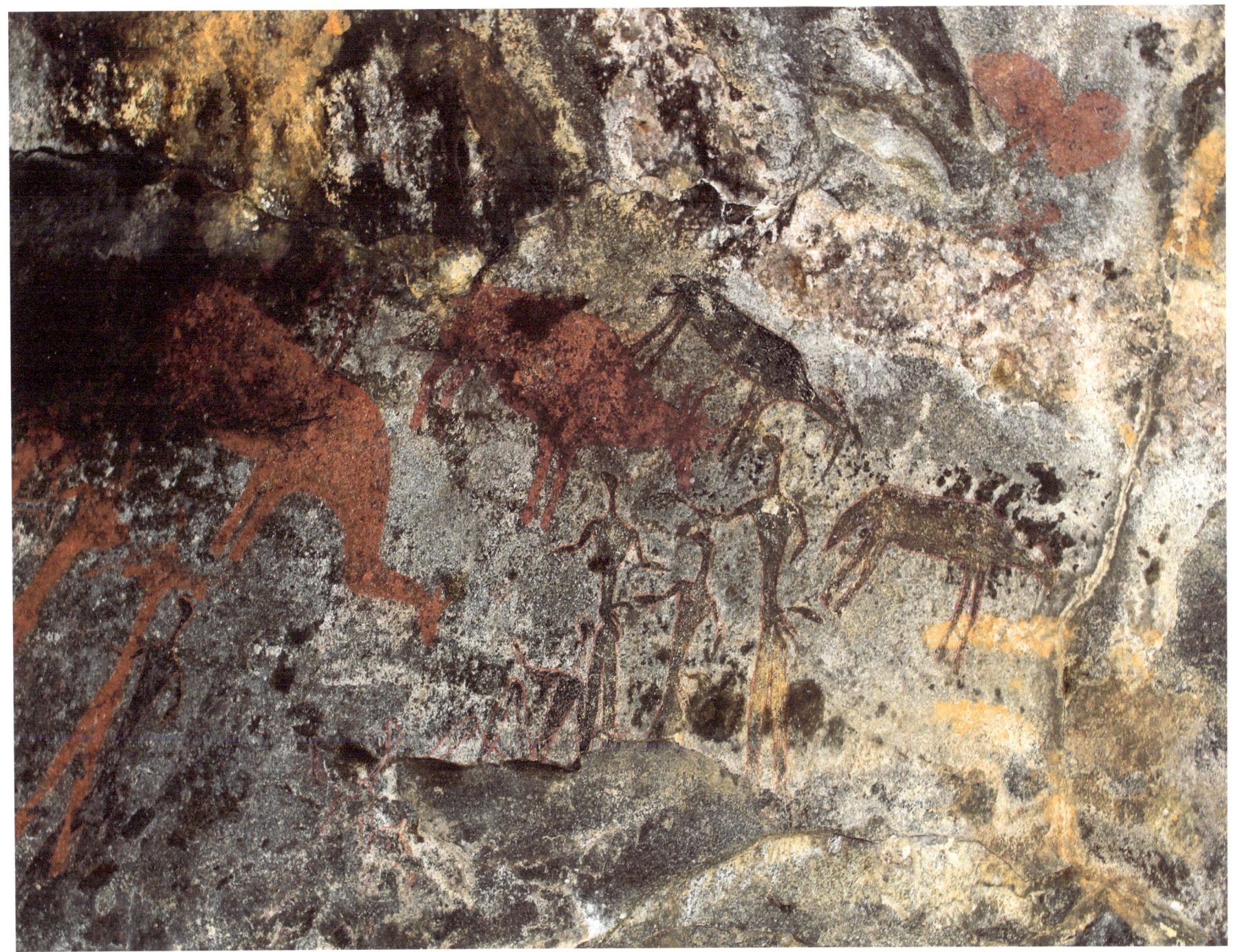

SOTHOS

The first black culture that can be clearly identified are the Sotho speaking peoples who arrived in Eswatini around 1000 years ago, or a little later. They came inland from the north and tended to settle on the highveld which had plentiful rains but poor, mineral leached soils. They built terraces and were able to use the same terraces for several hundred years by composting them, greatly increasing the soil fertility.

The highveld was largely treeless. Often, their huts were clustered around central, circular livestock enclosures. The domed hut structures are likely to have been made of saplings and grass.

In the mid 1500s the Portuguese established a small port for their Indian trading ships at what is now Maputo. The highveld Sotho started trading with them, using river valleys like the Komati as routes. They traded gold and ivory, probably for cloth and beads. By the early 1800s, numbers of people from varied tribal backgrounds were living and trading on the highveld. They probably spoke seSotho and are now known as the Bokoni.

Opposite: Mantjolo Pool, near Mbabane. Mantjolo is a sacred Sotho site and National Monument. Directions are on page 44.
Right: Sotho stone walling on a hilltop near Hawane.
Below: Sotho circular walling in the Londozi Valley.

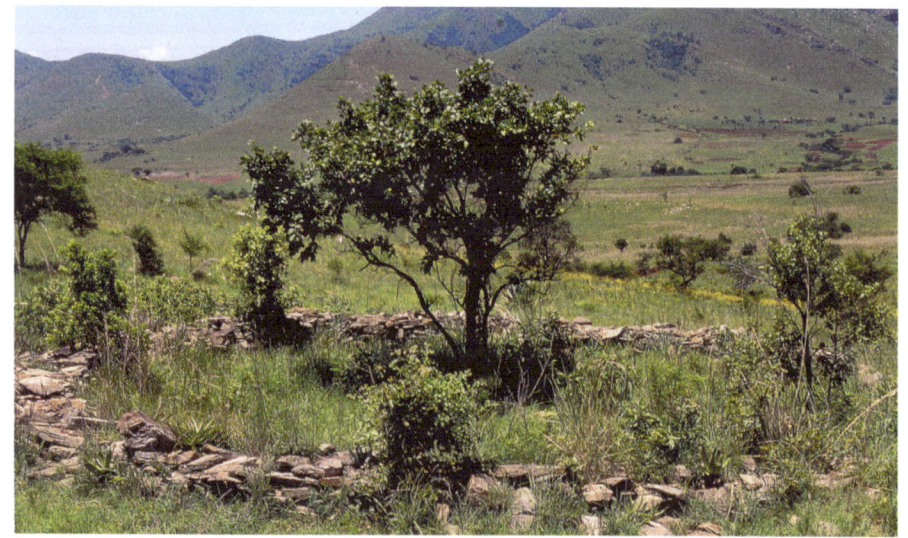

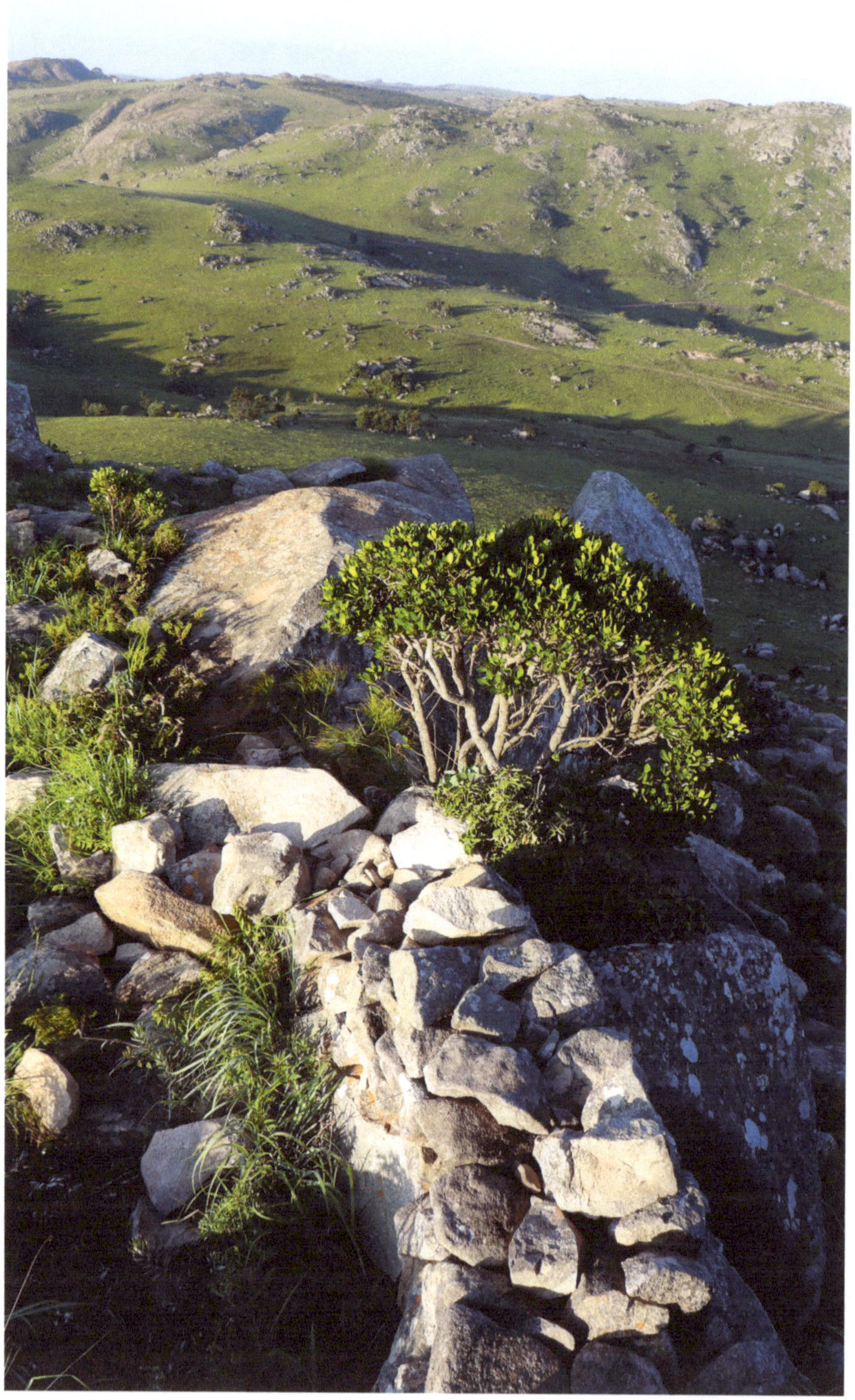

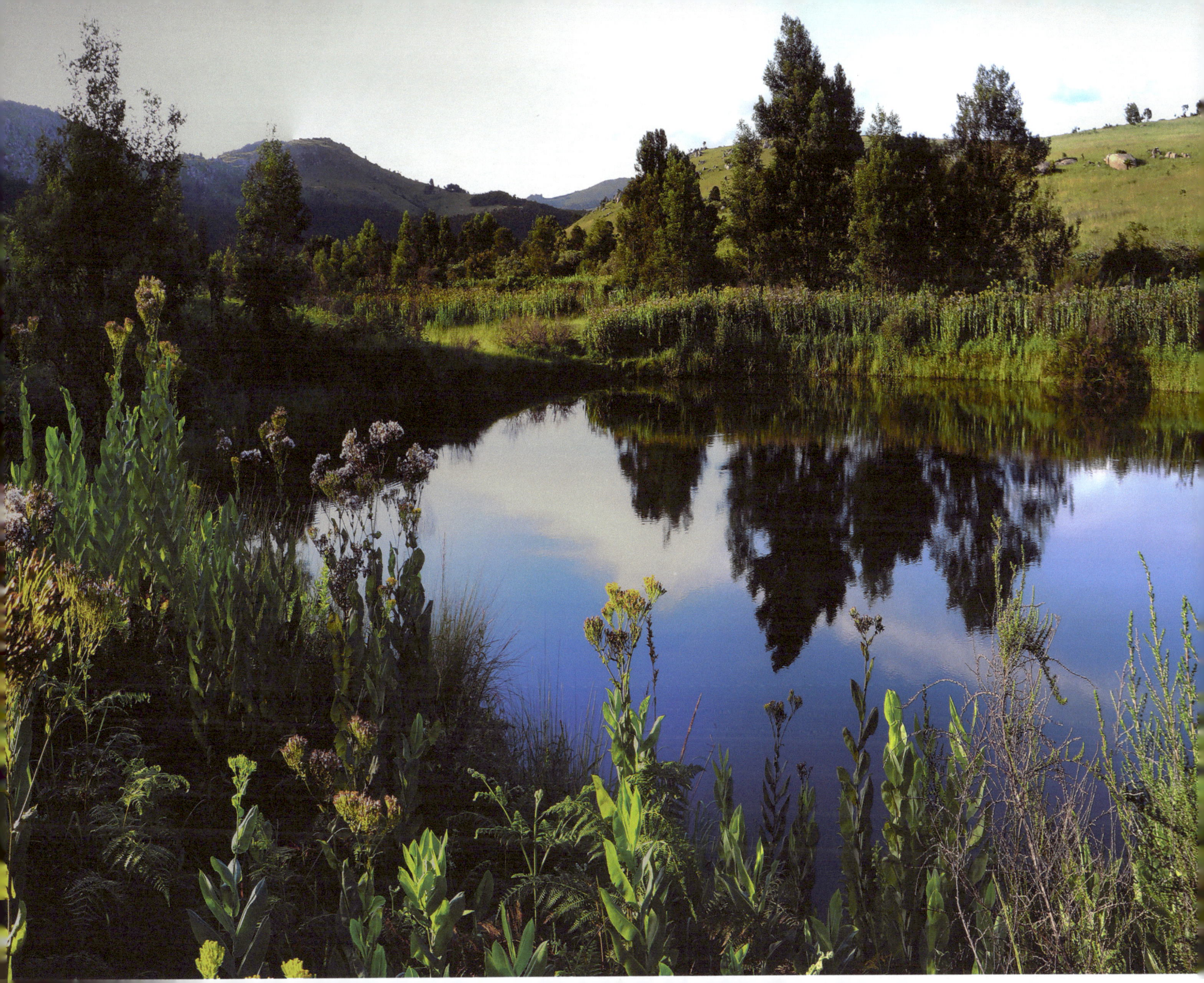

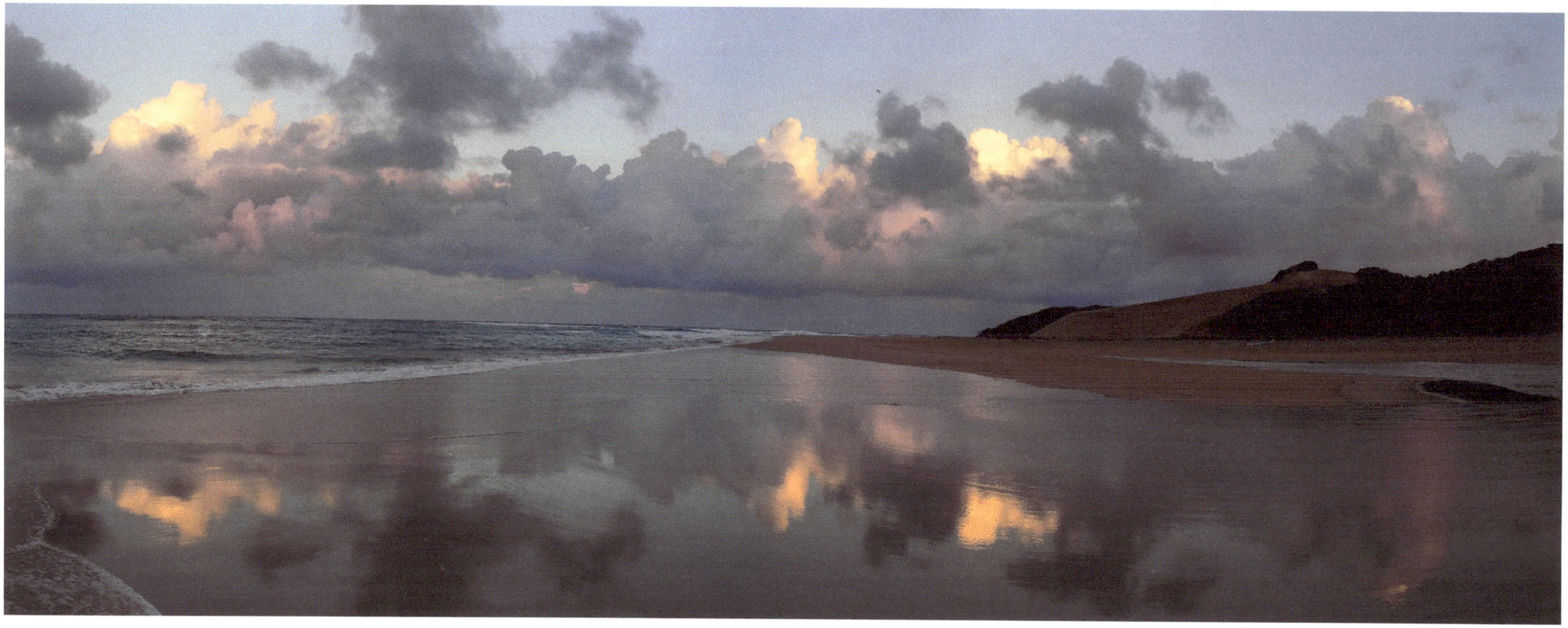

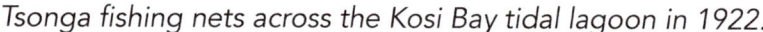

Seawater from Mozambique has deep ritual significance in Eswatini.

Tsonga fishing nets across the Kosi Bay tidal lagoon in 1922.

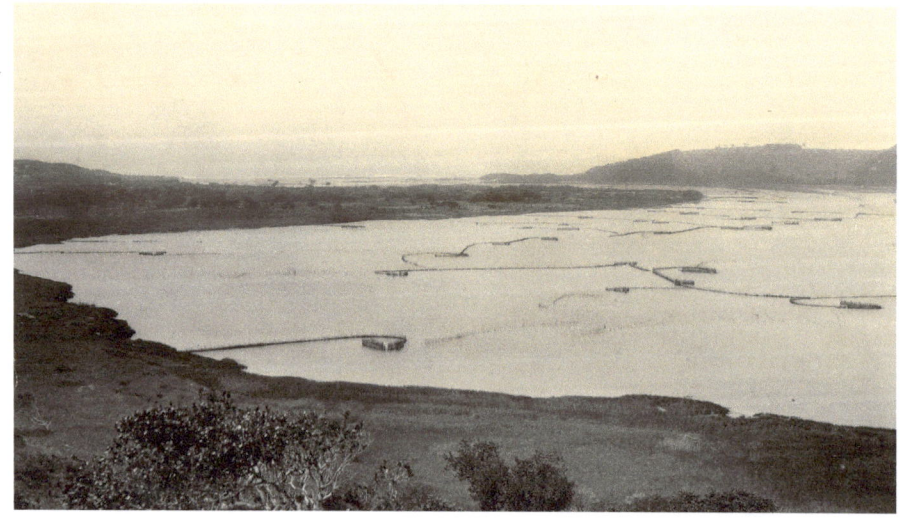

NGUNIS

The Nguni people slowly migrated down the east coast of Africa. Near the Zambezi they had long interactions with the San and acquired spoken clicks from them, as well as a few rituals. Some ancestral Nguni were cattle herders and did not fish. The sea, and seawater, were ritually important to them all.

One Nguni clan, the Dlaminis, had moved from the coast at kaTembe on Maputo Bay into the Pongola Valley, and then into the south of Eswatini by the mid 1750s. Around 1815 the aggressive Zulu empire was expanding, and the Dlamini led a clan alliance to resist Zulu armies. This military alliance formed the nucleus of the Swazi state and they adopted the Incwala ceremony which became a unifying celebration of the Dlamini kingship.

The resulting military kingdom, based on age group regiments, grew rapidly. They absorbed or conquered Sotho clans and expanded the boundaries of the kingdom. Some important Dlamini ritual sites remain on the coast, and people are sent to the sea annually to fetch seawater to start the *Incwala*.

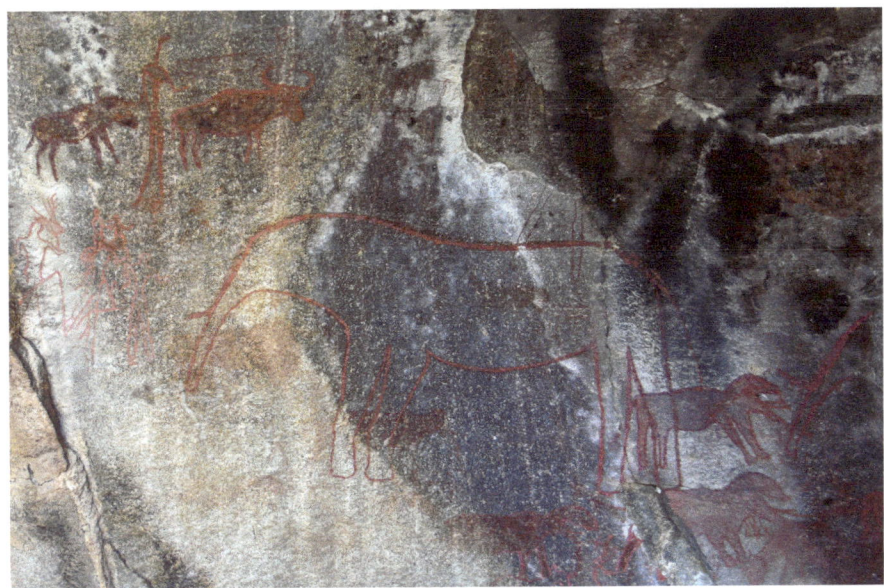

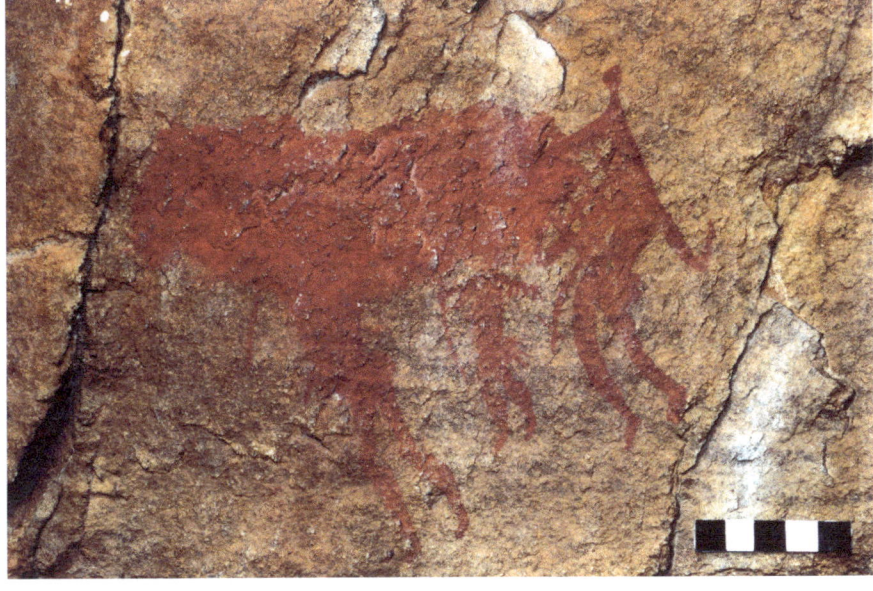

Above: An elephant at Nsangwini, with two rainbulls, bottom right.
Below: The Eswatini coat of arms on a coin.

People catching a rainbull with a net.

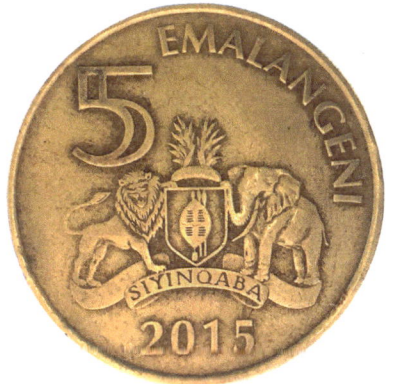

RAIN MAKING

The San believed that in order to make rain they needed to catch a rainbull with a net, shown above right. Once the rainbull had been caught, it could be controlled, and then so could the rain. Hippo-like rainbulls were encountered in the power reality and lived in large river pools. The painting above at Nsangwini shows two rainbulls at the bottom right corner.

ELEPHANTS and RAIN MAKING

Elephants are highly skilled at finding water during severe droughts. For this reason they probably came to symbolise rainmaking to the San. The Nsangwini rock art shelter is above a large placid pool on the Komati River, paintings of rainbulls and an elephant indicate that it is likely to have been a rainmaking site.

When the Dlamini were consolidating the Swazi state during the 19th century, they also needed to control rain making. They tried forcing Sotho chiefs, who had long been in contact with the San, to give up their rain making secrets.

The Dlamini had a dual gender monarchy, with both male and female leaders. Elephants symbolised the Dlamini female leader, one of whose main ritual roles was rainmaking, as well as providing political leadership if there was no male monarch - elephant herds are led by females.

Today the elephant symbolises the *Indlovukati*, or Great She Elephant, also known as the Queen Mother who rules in the absence of a King.

Directions to Nsangwini are on page 44.

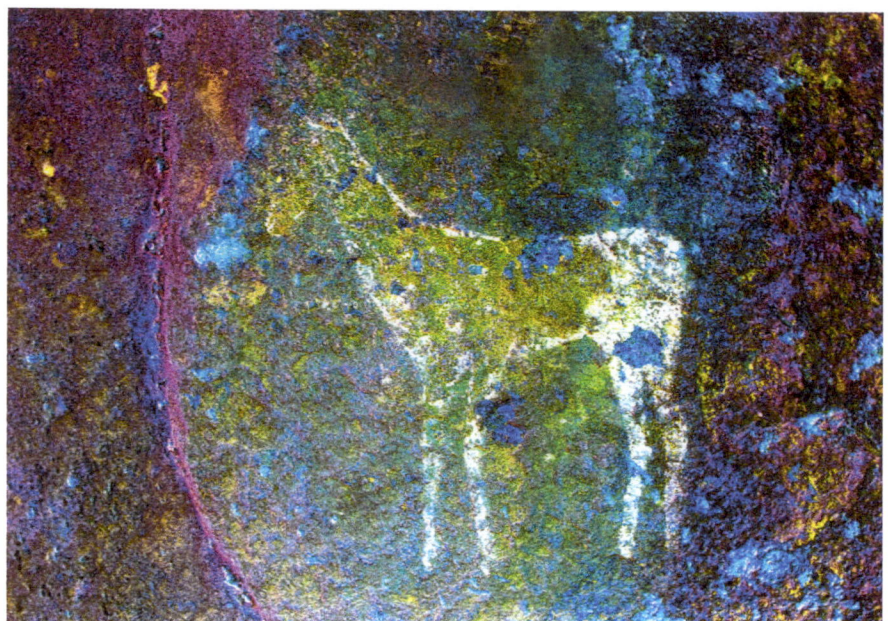

San painting, possibly of a horse. (DStretch image)

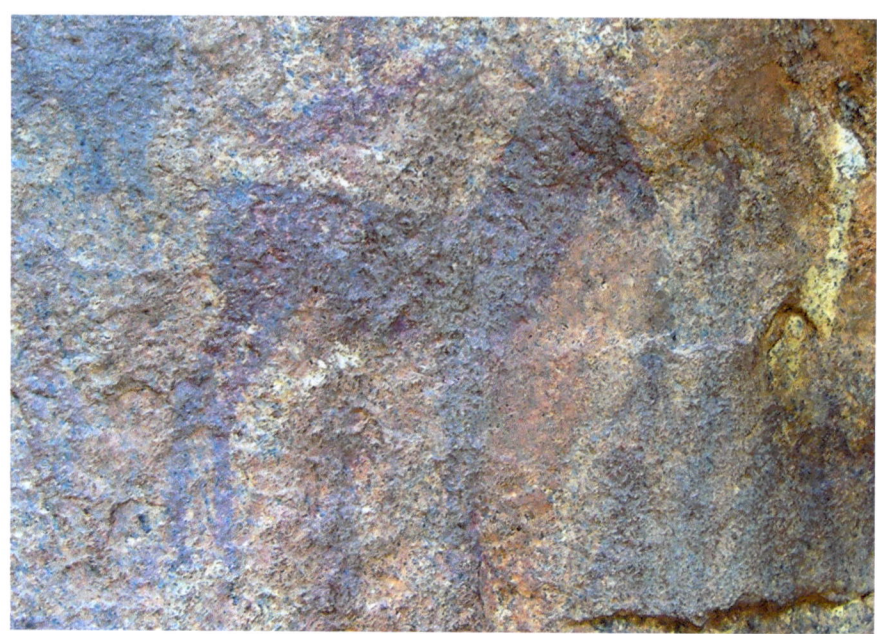

Possible painting of a mule.

WHEN WERE THE LAST SAN IN ESWATINI?

We don't know, but there are clues. There were San just south of Eswatini in the late 1800s, and also to the west at Lake Chrissie where they survived well into the 1950s. Swazi clan traditions speak of 'clearing' the land of San as the Swazi state expanded from south to north in the early and mid 1800s.

In the 1950s an elderly man informed Johnny Masson, the first researcher of archaeology in the country, that his grandfather had been tasked by the Dlamini to kill the San so that it would be suitable for settlement by cattle owning Dlamini Swazis and their allies.

A mid-1800s land concession treaty between Swazis and Boers to the north provided the Boers with two options, 'cleared of prickles' or as it was, with San.

There may be evidence in the paintings themselves. The photo on the left may be a horse. Horses were introduced by colonials and could not have been seen earlier. The painting above has been interpreted as a mule, again this is not certain, but the style is not typical of any other animals, and mules were only introduced during the colonial era.

The first colonial settlement, by missionaries, was in 1844. No colonial documents mention the San. There is a reliable account of a single San man living in a very small hut next to a Swazi homestead in Pigg's Peak during the 1950s.

The San heritage certainly continues genetically in high cheekboned, light skinned people in the country. It also has influenced siSwati in spoken clicks, and in some rituals and beliefs.

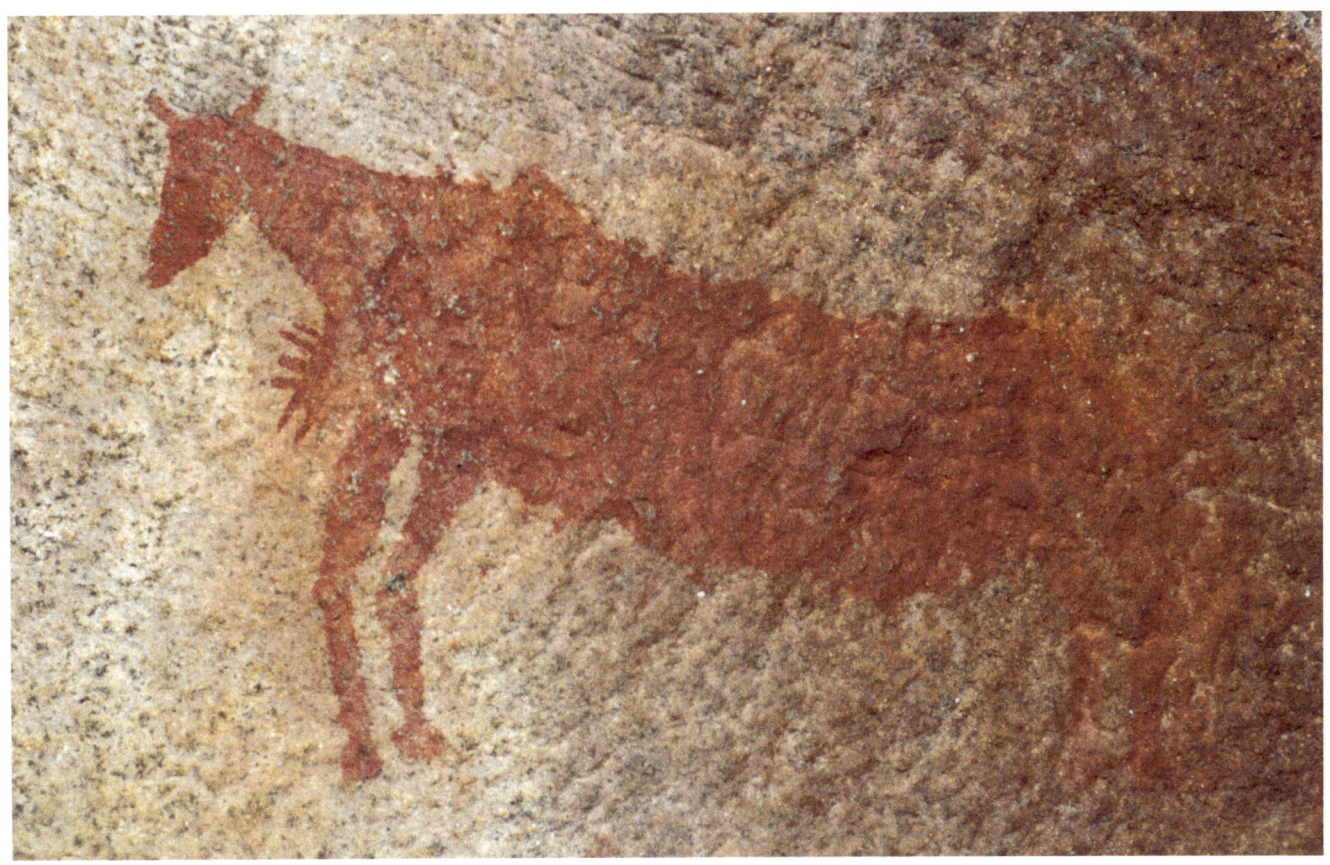

Antelope with anatomically accurate external heart.

MOUNTAIN REFUGES

For many thousands of years the San would have lived in the middleveld. It combines fertile grass for animals, water and a warm, mist-free climate without malaria or Tsetse Fly. For the same reasons, this was also the zone of choice for black settler-farmers. The resulting competition for land would have favoured the farmers with superior technology and a more complex and aggressive society. The San would have been marginalised into the high mountains above the landscape that they had previously inhabited.

These areas were not suitable for cattle farming, as a result, the San could continue their hunter-gatherer lifestyle there without competition. The majority of paintings in Eswatini are in the highveld, or in rocky river valleys.

San marginalisation occured in other parts of southern Africa before the colonial era. The San were isolated in areas like the Drakensberg which was too cold and wet for cattle, and the Kalahari which was too hot and dry.

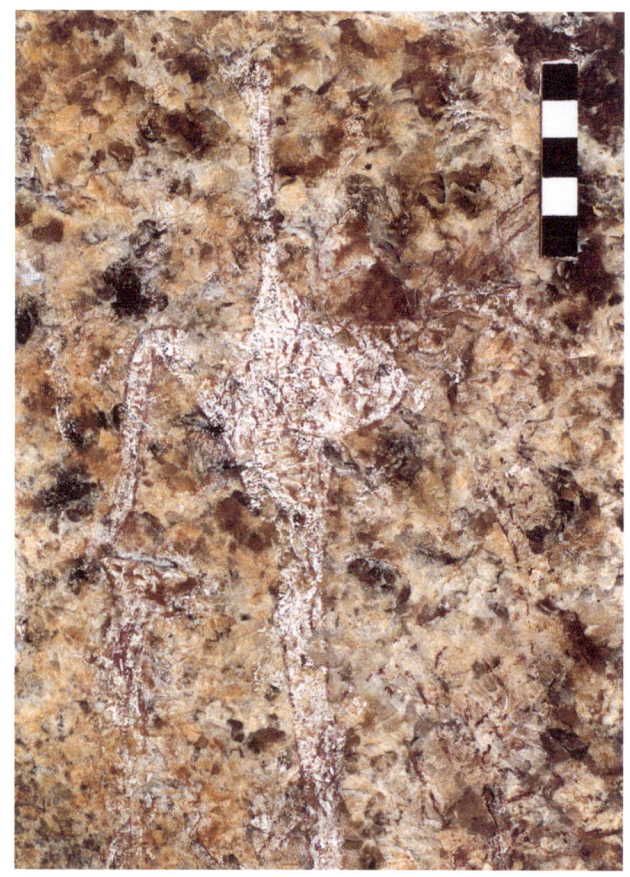 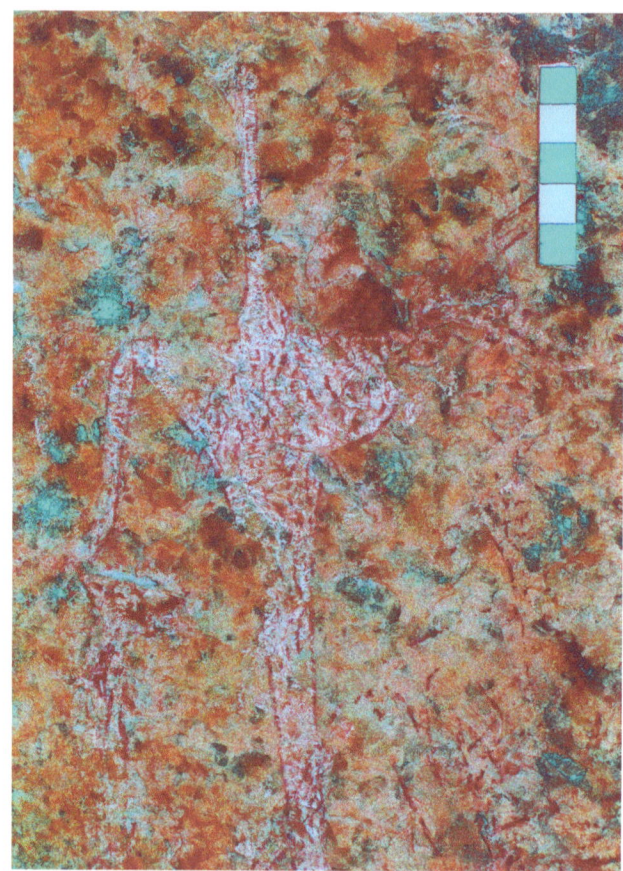

Late period painting of a male torso with ochre and white body paint, enhanced version on the right.

ZIONISM WORLDWIDE

In the late 1800s, a worldwide evangelical faith-healing movement began rejecting western medicine and focused on healing by the Christian Holy Spirit channeled through trance. They took their authority from a re-reading of the gospels which described speaking in tongues and faith healing. The healing movement started in Australia and then spread to working class communities in the United States. Zion City in Illinois was established and followers became known as Zionists. From the US it spread to Johannesburg in 1904 as "Zion". The first black Zionist missionary was a South African born Swazi, Daniel Nkonyane. His first convert was a Swazi, Johanna Ndwandwe.

ZIONISM IN SWAZILAND

Johanna Ndwandwe's sister was Lomawa, mother of the future King Sobhuza. She introduced Daniel Nkonyane to the Swazi royal family and he was credited with miraculously restoring Queen Mother Gwamile's failing eyesight. Afterwards, Gwamile supported Zionism which fused Christian and traditional Swazi beliefs, and was free from colonial influence.

Swazi Zionism evolved rapidly. Without any central control, new churches formed around charismatic healer-prophets. Circular San-like trance dances were adopted and some ancient San sacred places were used for Zionist rituals and ceremonies.

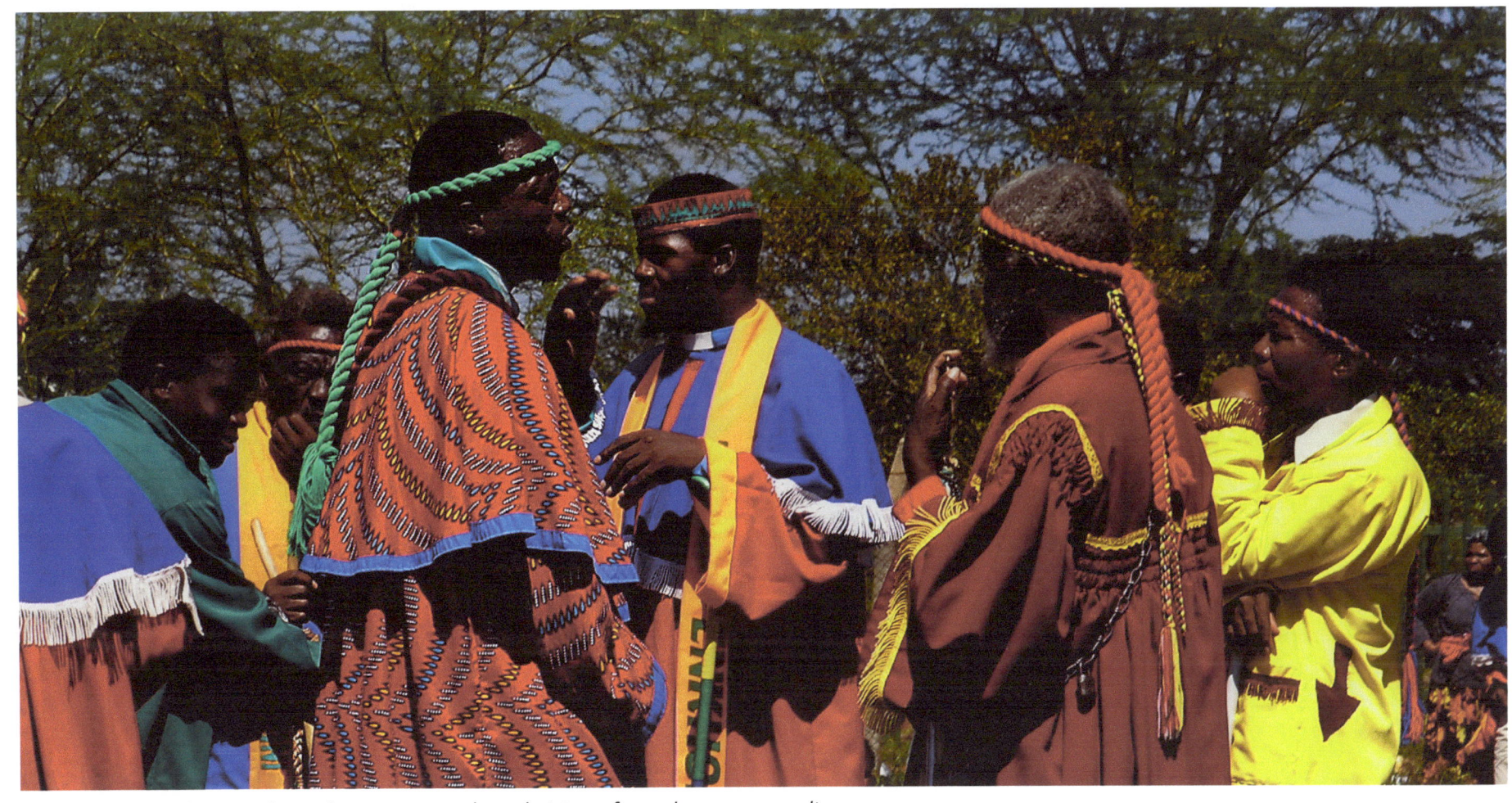

Some Zionist robes are based on trance induced visions from the power reality.

WATERFALLS and SACRED POOLS

Large, still pools of water were places of power to the San, and paintings are sometimes associated with them. The power associated with sacred pools has been appropriated into Swazi culture and some sites sacred to the San are now sacred to Zionists. They hold weekly trance rituals at these sites, particularly where waterfalls drop into large pools. Traditional Swazi and Zulu cosmology holds that the world is made of earth, wind, fire and water. Waterfalls are where earth, wind and water combine.

For some Zionists, when fire is ceremonially added, the four elements fuse and creation power is unleashed. Candle wax is often found near waterfalls and deep river pools, after night ceremonies.

CULTURAL CONTINUITY

The painting of three eland on page 10 is close to a large deep pool with a waterfall. Zionists regularly trance dance beneath the painting. The nearby sacred pool and waterfall is visited by thousands of colourfully robed Zionists on annual pilgrimages.

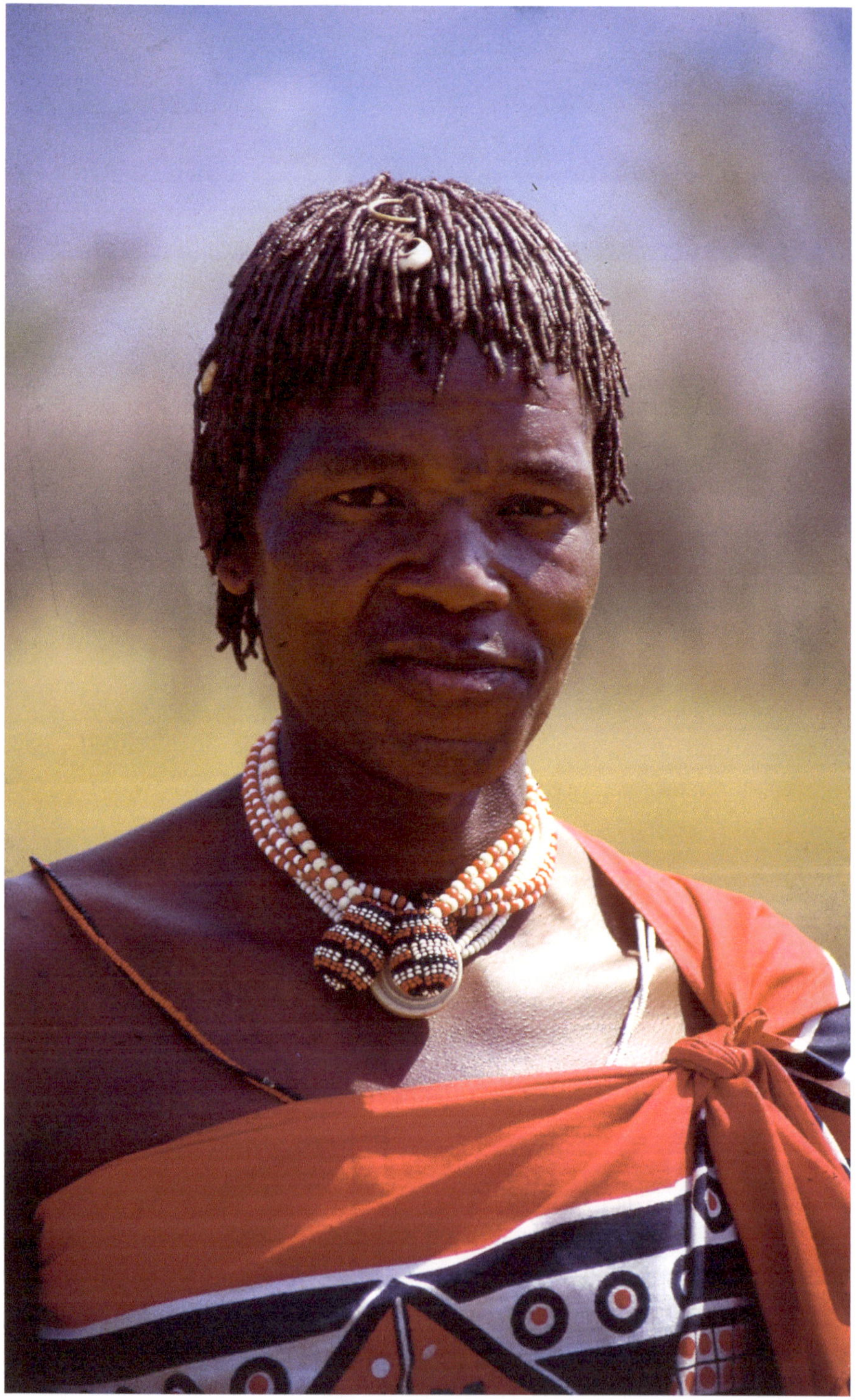

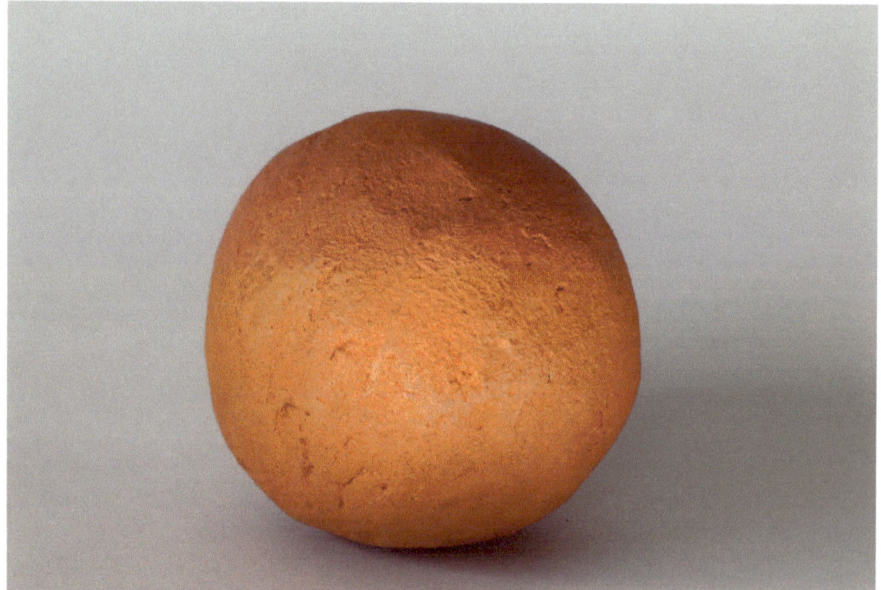

Left: A sangoma, or traditional healer with ochre in his hair.
Above: Balls of ochre are commonly sold at markets.
Right: A cloth wrap with a pattern only worn by traditional healers.

OCHRE and TRADITIONAL HEALERS

In the Swazi traditional view illness and misfortune are often brought about by people disrespecting their ancestors or by jealousy, spells, or discord in the ancestral realm.

The difficulty is in determining the precise cause. After years of training, *tangoma* (singular - *sangoma*), believe that they are able to hear the voice of a guiding ancestral spirit who informs them of the real cause of the patient's illness or misfortune, and provides a remedy. The ancestor brings about the healing, not the sangoma who is a conduit.

The ancestral connection is enhanced by wearing ochre mixed with fat in the hair. The ochre helps to lower the veil between the power reality and ordinary life. Ochre can also be used instead of a small sacrifice, like a chicken, in order to get the ancestor's attention.

Red, black and white are the three main colours in San rock art, they are also the colours that symbolise traditional healers. Ritually, ochre is blood.

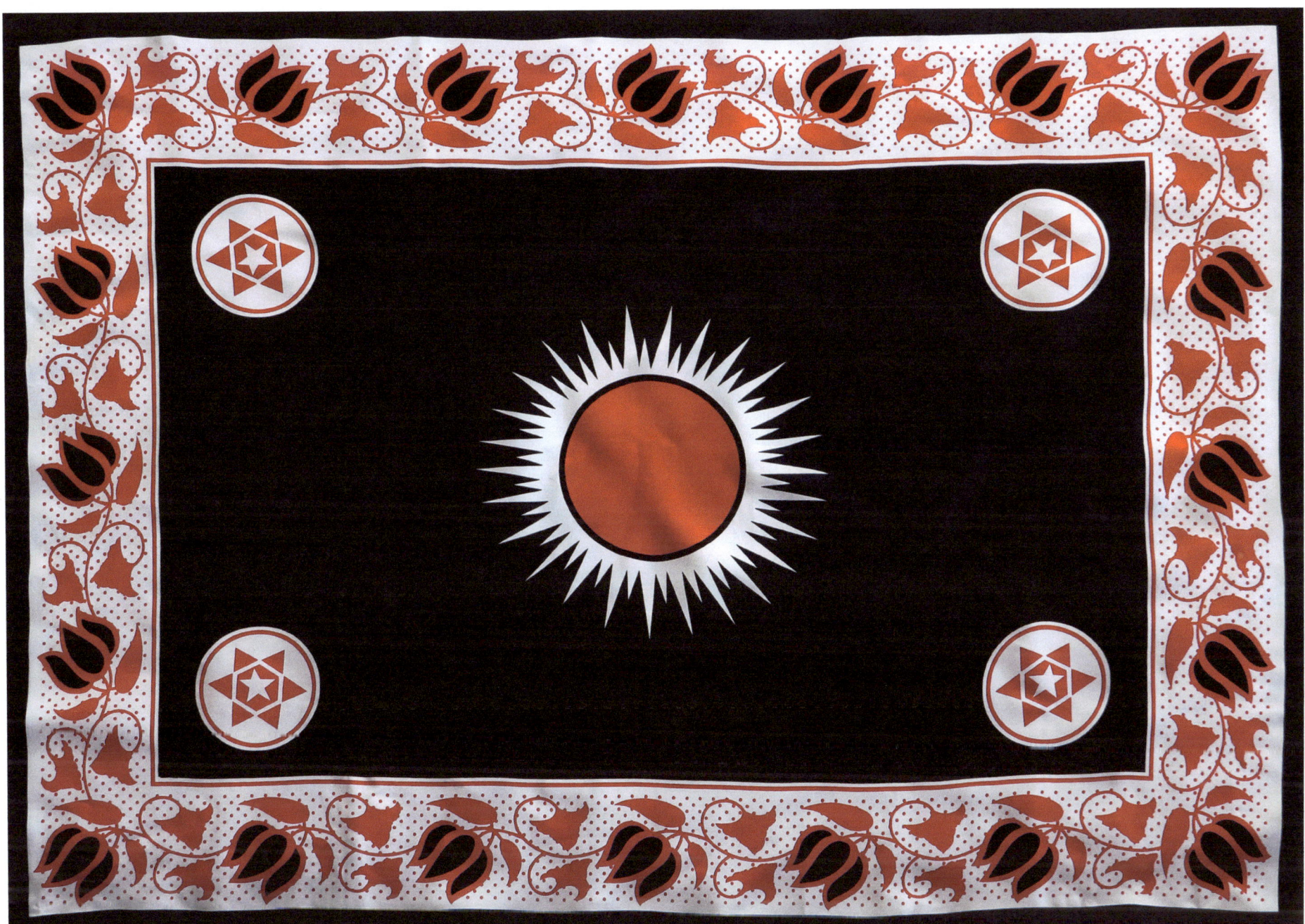

33

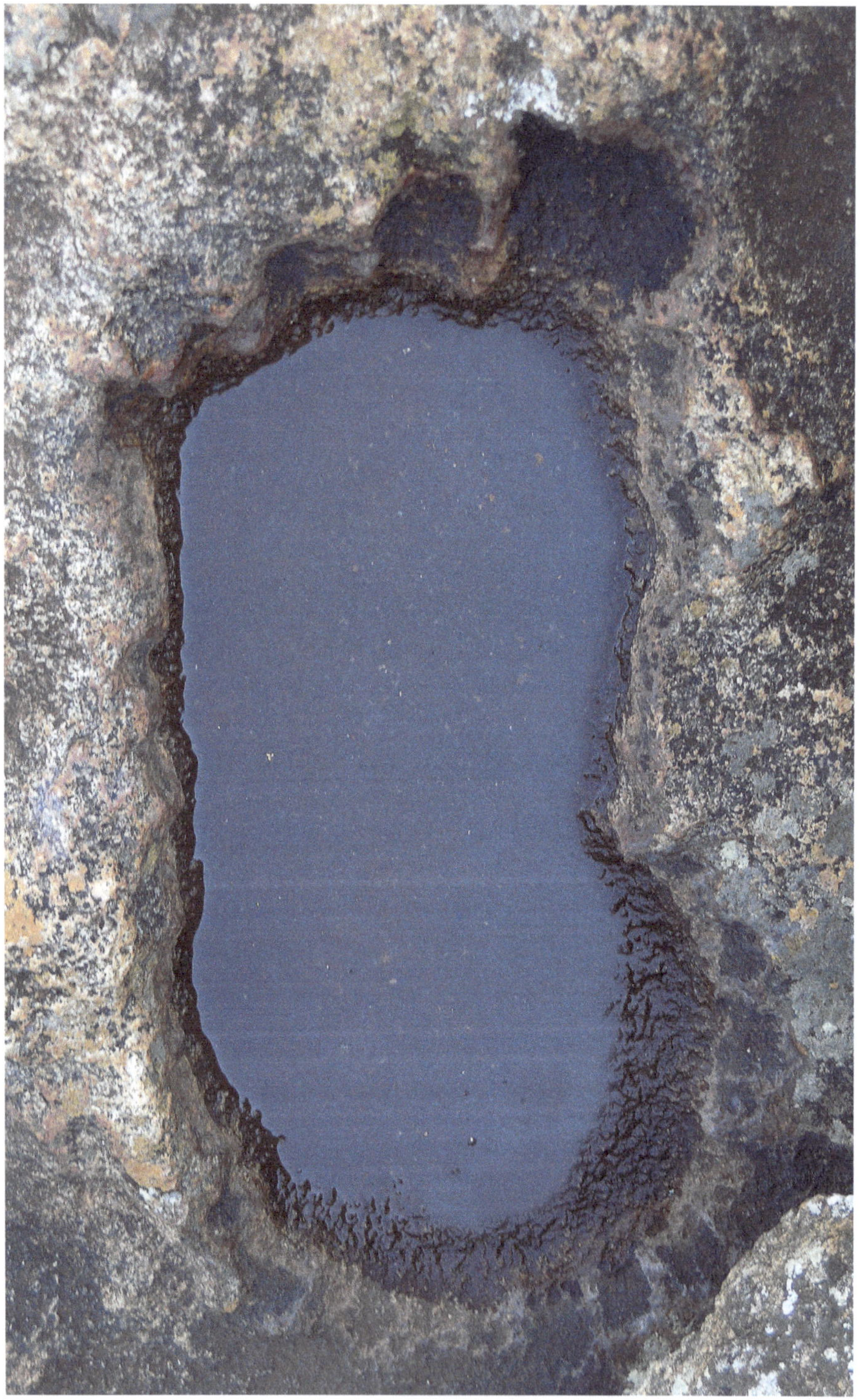

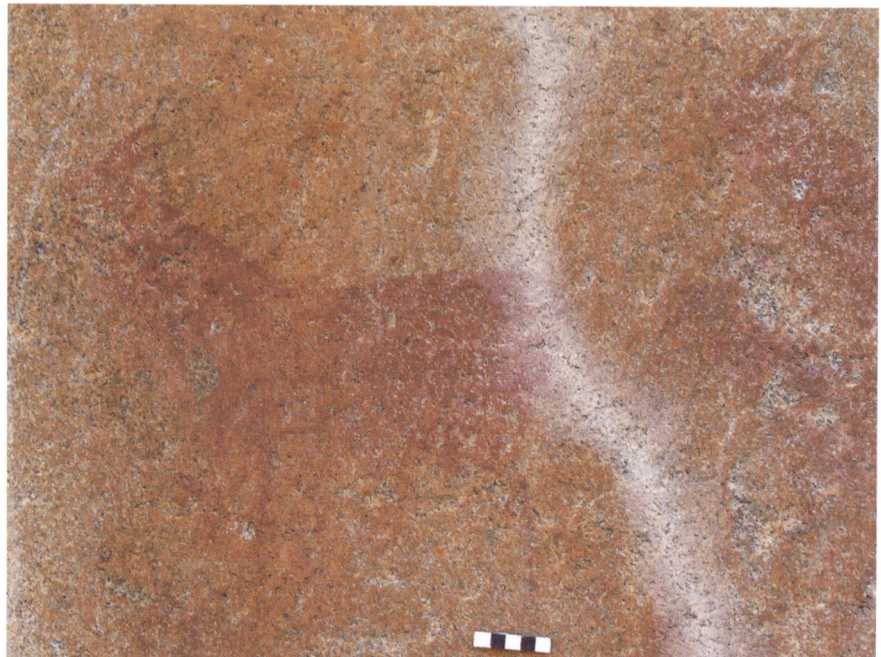

Above: A very faint San red ochre painting of eland at Ntfonjeni.
Left: God's footprint in granite at Ntfonjeni.

ECHOES THROUGH TIME

In northeastern Eswatini a cultural tradition stretches from the stone ages to the present. Like much of the country, the rocks around Ntfonjeni are granite. Weathering and erosion in granite sometimes starts off as small depressions that fill with water and slowly widen. There are potentially millions of combinations of erosion depressions possible, some small, others several metres across. Many are interlinked forming random patterns. Very occasionally natural erosion in granite looks like a human footprint, with each toe shown.

These rare rock footprints were recognised by early people and explanations accumulated around them. Before science began several hundred years ago, mythic explanations for natural phenomena were common to cultures worldwide.

We know that the San considered the footprint at Ntfonjeni as a place of power, as the closest suitable rock surface has paintings. Though faint, several red ochre eland are discernable. What we don't know is whether or not the concept of a one legged creator god was started by the San, or if it had other origins.

Swazi cosmology has a single creator god, *Mlentengamunye*, the One Legged One. Occasionally he left a single footprint behind when creating the world at a time when rock was still soft. When the rock hardened, the footprints were preserved forever.

It is possible that conceptually the single legged creator god had one foot in this reality and the other in the power reality, a view that would make intuitive sense to shamanic people.

The footprint was a place of power for the San, but was later appropriated as a military base, remaining a sacred site of considerable power for the rapidly expanding Swazi nation from the early 1850s to 1868 under King Mswati II.

Ntfonjeni became the northernmost permanent Swazi royal settlement. Impis of warriors would go northwards primarily to raid for cattle and captives before returning, although some remained behind and founded Swazi communties that still exist in South Africa.

When Mswati II died he was buried in the south, but his weapons were buried near Ntfonjeni, so that his power and influence would be spread evenly over the land. Over one and a half centuries after Mswati II's death in 1868, traditional regiments at major events and ritual ceremonies dance their history and chant the following:

We will never leave Ntfonjeni
We guard the foot
Of the Great First One.

Asiyuhamba eNtfonjeni
Tsine sagadza lunyawo
IwaMkhulunchanti, tsine.

Today the royal *umphakatsi* or homestead of Ntfonjeni has resident soldiers from the regiments. The site is easily accessible and is open to the public.

Directions are on page 44.

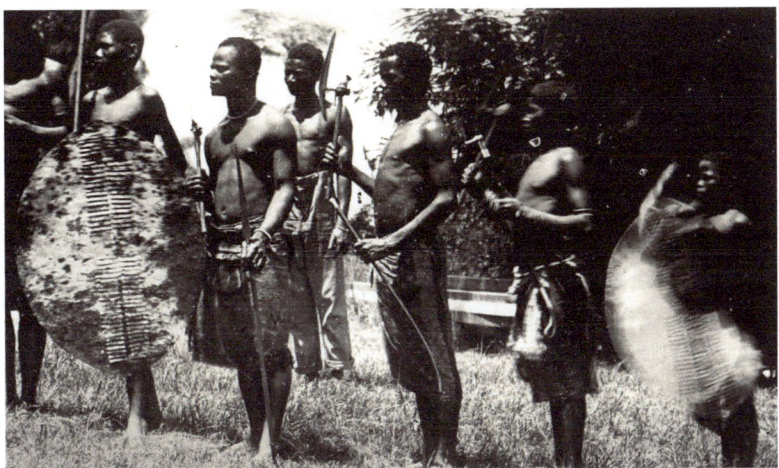

Swazi warriors in 1895 at Mbekelweni. Note the large, but heavy, battle shields that provided almost total body protection to a crouching person.

Swazi warriors in the 1920s, a generation after the last war. They carry lighter, smaller, ceremonial dancing shields.

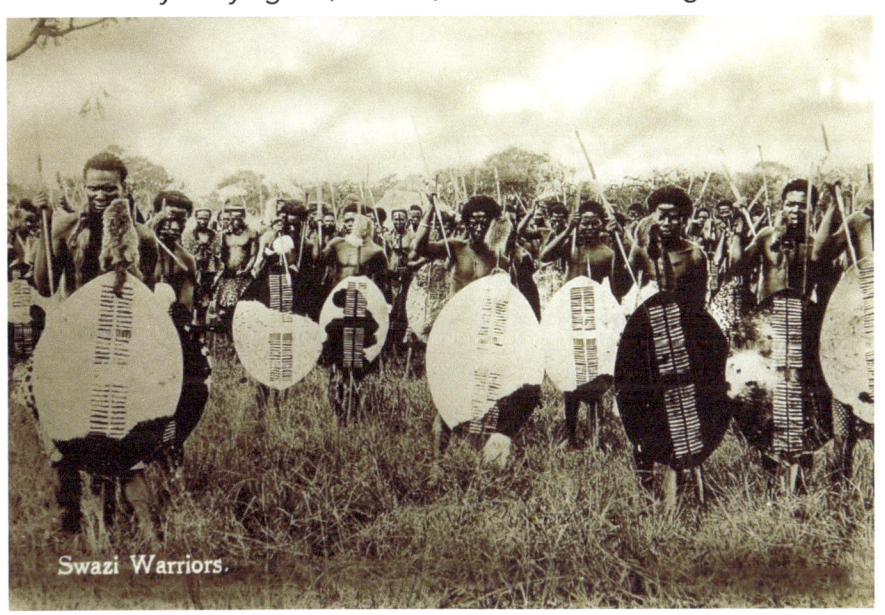

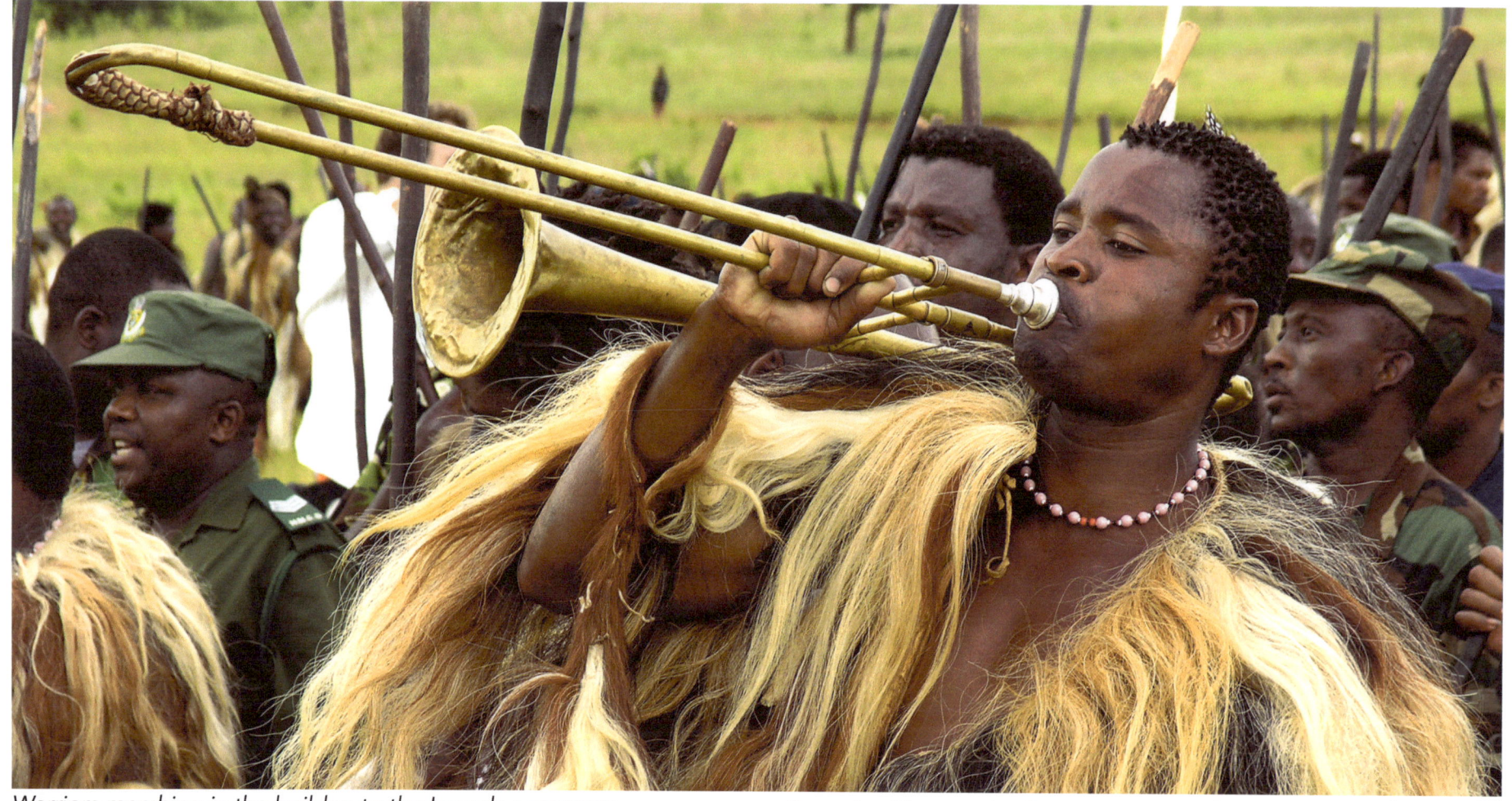

Warriors marching in the buildup to the Incwala ceremony.

Opposite: Thousands of young men march in preparation for Incwala.

SWAZI TRADITION

In 1903 Swaziland was incorporated into the British Empire, despite British guarantees of perpetutual independence signed two decades earlier. This caused a crisis for the Swazi leadership, particularly for King Sobhuza II who became ruler of the nation in 1921. He soon became disillusioned with British justice. After a period of reflection, he increasingly emphasized traditional Swazi values in order to resist colonialism.

From the mid 1930s onwards, the king often went barefoot, wore traditional clothes and lived frugally. He was always trying to get more land for Swazis, and gradually increased the power of the chiefs over whom he had authority.

Between the 1930s and Independence in 1968 he consolidated his political power. After Independence, Swazi National Traditionalism became the dominant political policy under his absolute rule, and remains so. Many cultural forms that have disappeared, or been marginalised in other African countries, are mainstream in Eswatini.

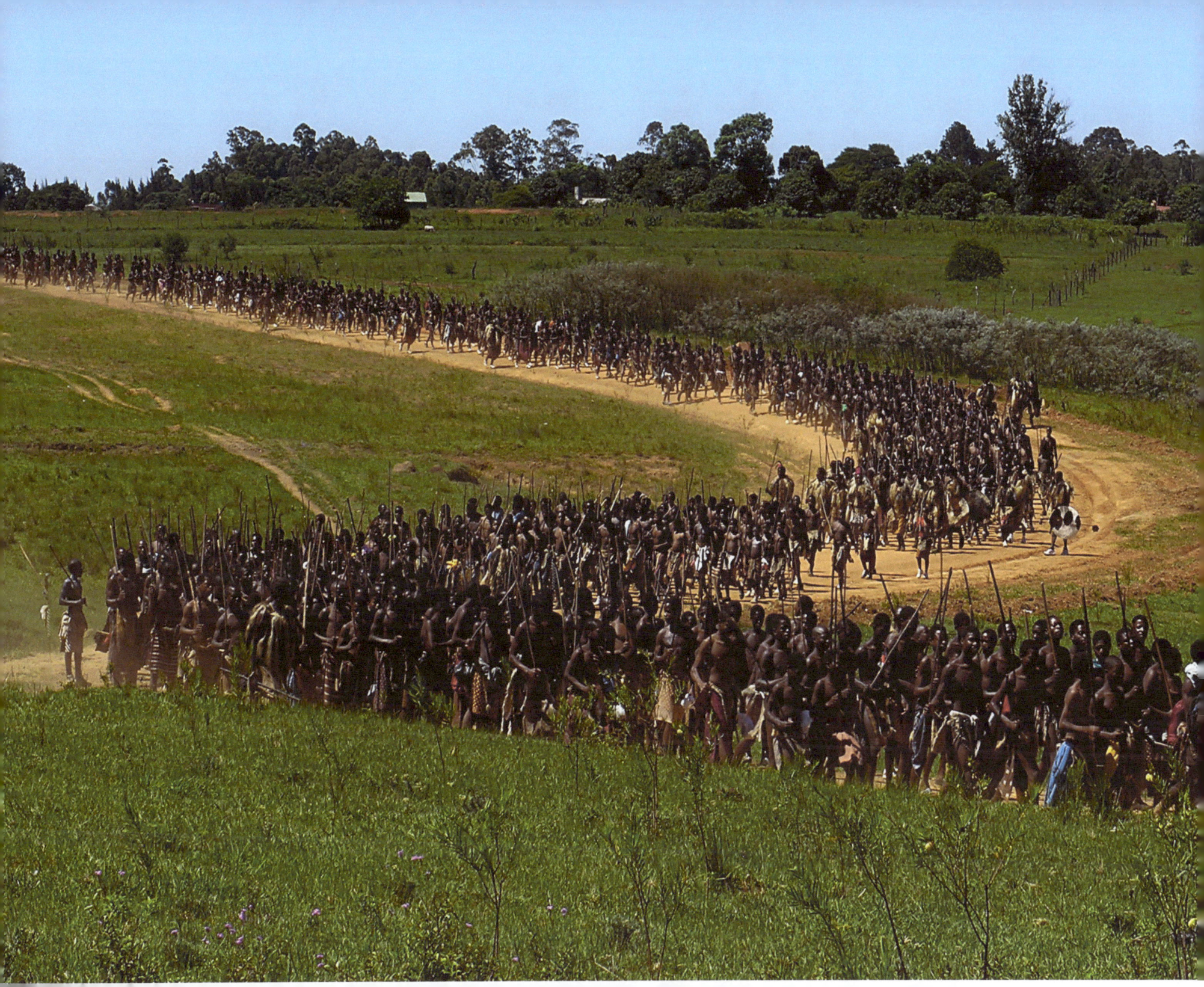

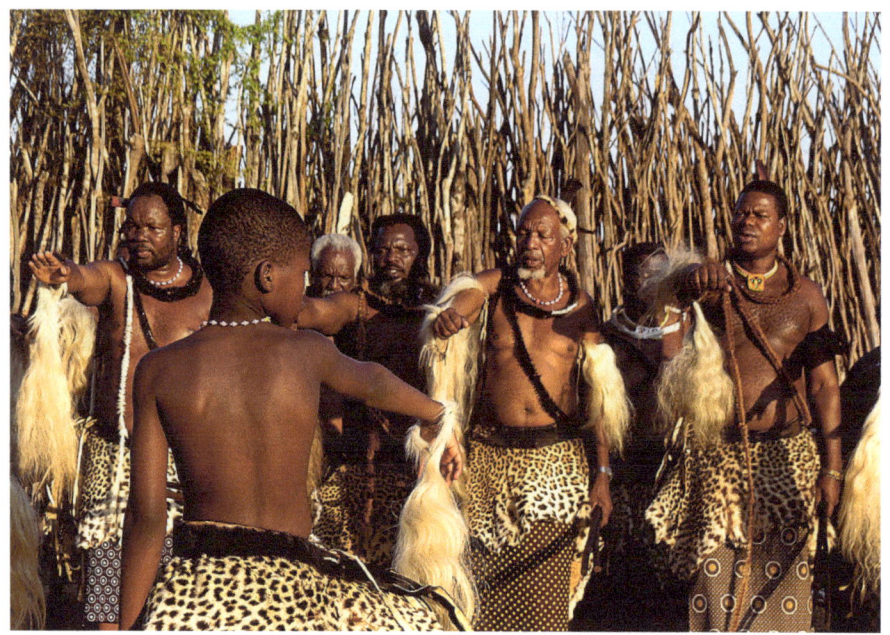
Warriors and children practising for the Incwala.

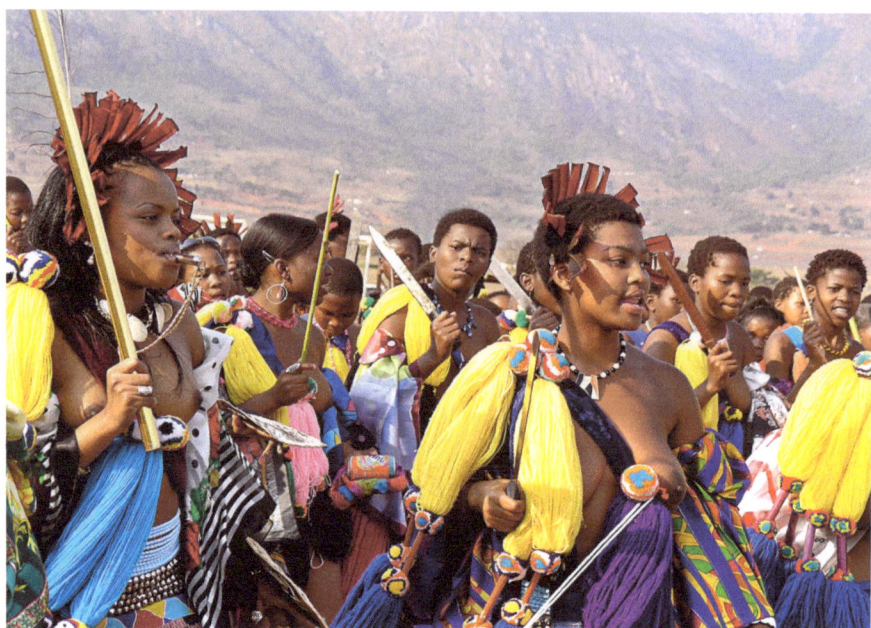
Princesses dancing at the Umhlanga.

INCWALA

This annual kingship ceremony is recognised as one of only two major African ceremonies to survive colonialism intact. It was first held in Eswatini by King Sobhuza I in the early 1800s, and helped consolidate the emerging Swazi state under Dlamini leadership.

The ceremony itself has several smaller rituals within it, and is part public and part private, starting with the *Bemanti* or water people, being sent to Mozambique to fetch sea water.

After their return, tens of thousands of youths then march from a royal residence to fetch *lusekwane* (sacred bushes) to build a shelter for the king, as shown on the previous page.

Days of complex ceremonies follow, the main day is dramatic, with tens of thousands of chanting warriors in full traditional battle dress.

The *Incwala* ends with the king and the nation having been purified from the past year's negativity and ritually strenghtened for the year ahead. The public are permitted to attend the main day.

UMHLANGA

For centuries young girls would be released to marry along with their agemate leader, usually the daughter of a chief or the king in a small local dance ceremony, the *umcwasho*.

In the mid 1930s, King Sobhuza II decided to group these many ceremonies together into a single national festival, this was the start of the *Umhlanga*. Unmarried girls and young women collected reeds and brought them to the Queen Mother to repair her residence. The festival provided a female counterpoint to the ancient male oriented *Incwala*.

Missionaries strongly opposed the *Umhlanga*, and the revealing dancing costumes, fearing 'a return to heathendom' and the king was unable to turn it into an annual ceremony. The next *Umhlanga* was held when thousands of soldiers returned after WW II needing wives, but the king was still not in a strong enough position to make it an annual ceremony. It was part of the first Independence celebrations in 1968 and since then *Umhlanga* has been an annual event with up to 100 000 young women participating. The public are welcome.

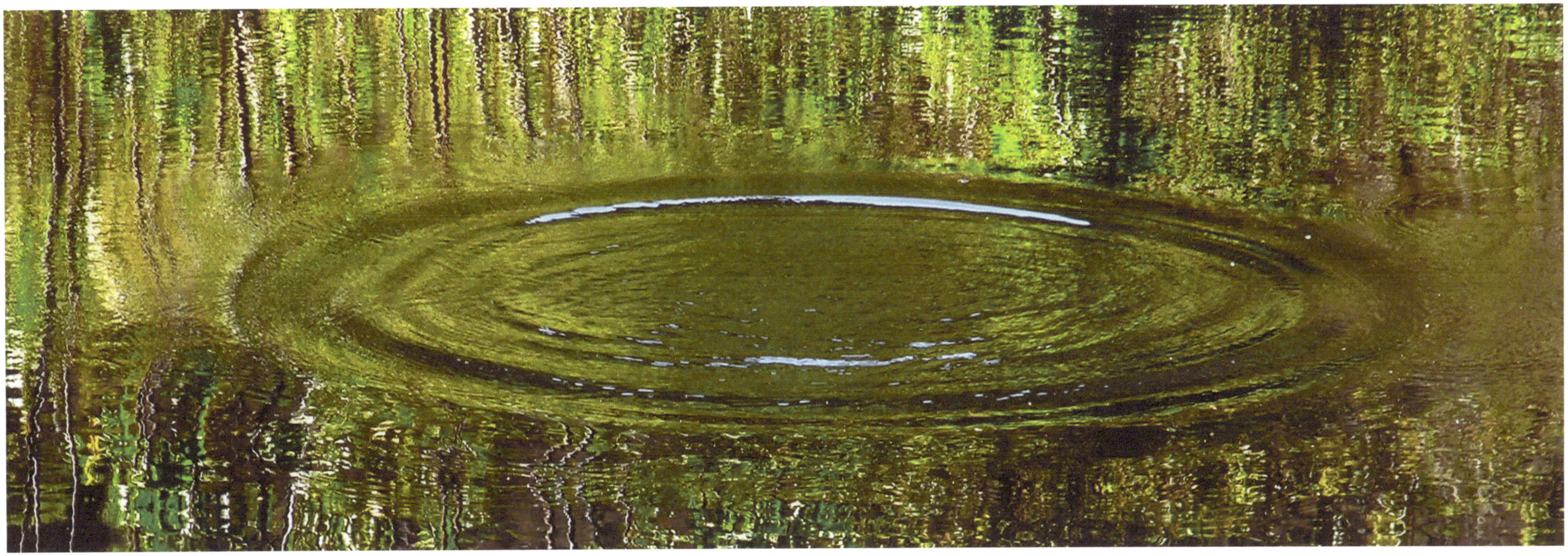

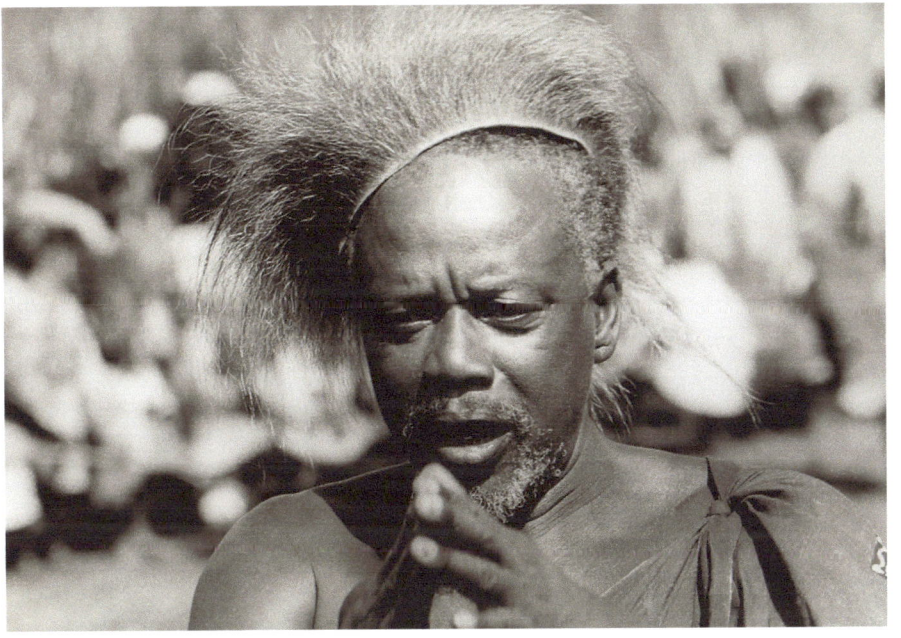

Pools of deep still water are places of power countrywide.

The Bemanti, or water people, fetch seawater from the coast to begin the Incwala. They wear distinctive baboon fur headgear.

OCHRE SUMMARY

Ochre runs like a red thread through time, linking past and present. Mining began at Ngwenya 43 000 years ago - and ochre is still collected there today. The San used ochre to connect with the power reality - and painted their experiences in ochre, often mixed with the blood of their totem animal, the eland.

San influence remains in the clicks in Bantu languages, in sacred pools, in rainmaking, in divination, in shamanic fly-whisks, in circular trance dances and in a few faded paintings evoking a way of life from thousands of years ago.

Today shamanic healers sometimes sprinkle a little ochre to summon the ancestors instead of sacrificing a chicken. For them, ochre is blood. Sometimes the ochre is from Ngwenya.

In traditional Swazi marriages the bride is smeared with ochre from her husband's homestead in the *teka* ceremony, allowing her husband's ancestors to connect to her. Ochre use from Ngwenya is the world's longest known spiritual tradition in one location.

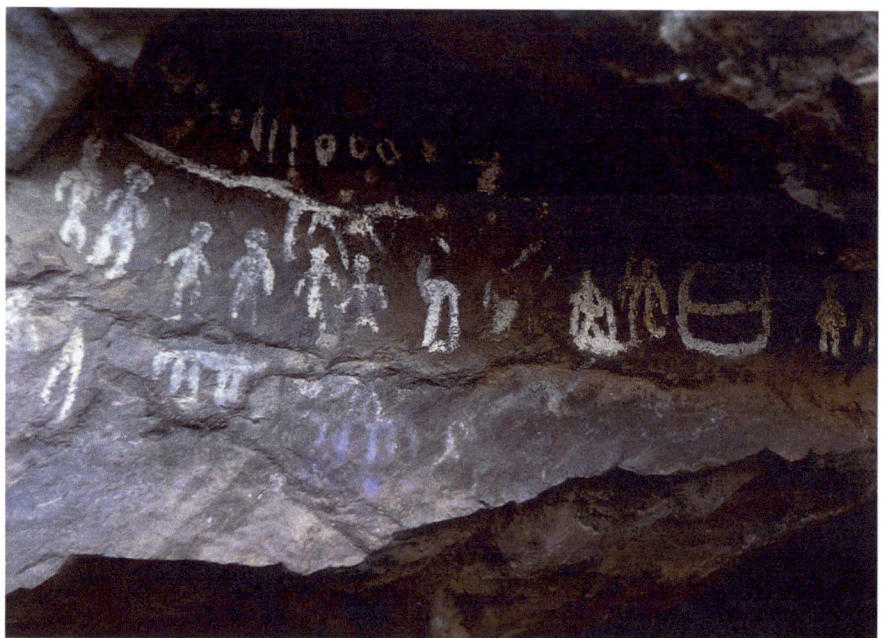

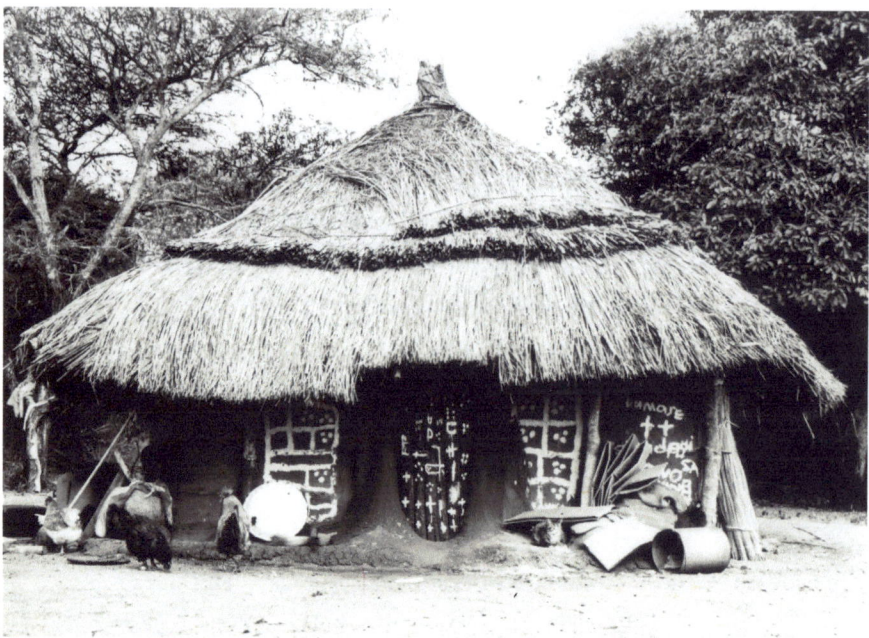

Above and below: Black Rock Art.

Painted Tsonga hut.

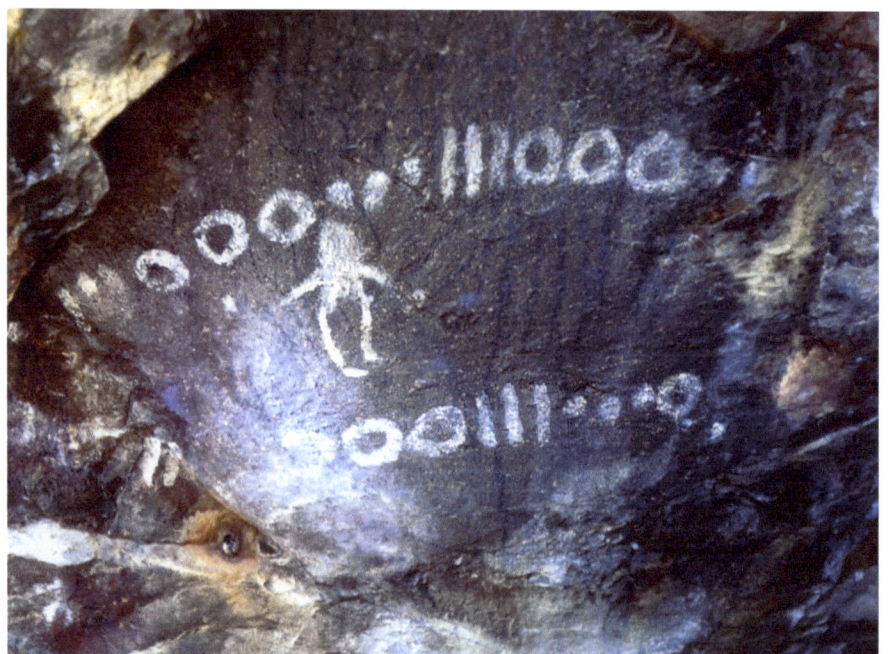

NON-OCHRE PAINTINGS

Many black southern African cultures have complex graphic traditions, but they are seldom representational. Instead, they tend towards geometric patterns, these are best expressed by the Ndebele who create wonderfully complex designs on houses and other objects.

In Eswatini there is only one known black painting site, in the Lubombo mountains, close to the Mozambican border. We know that the paintings are at least 120 years old because there is a carefully engraved colonial era signature with a convenient date near them. There are two friezes, both shown on the left.

Johnny Masson believed that they probably were associated with a Tsonga circumcision site. Tsonga people live on the nearby Mozambican coastal plains and used remote places for circumcision ceremonies. They also settled and farmed extensively near Simunye in pre-colonial times before the first Dlamini entered the country. Their tradition of white paint on dark backgrounds continues on the painted Tsonga hut above.

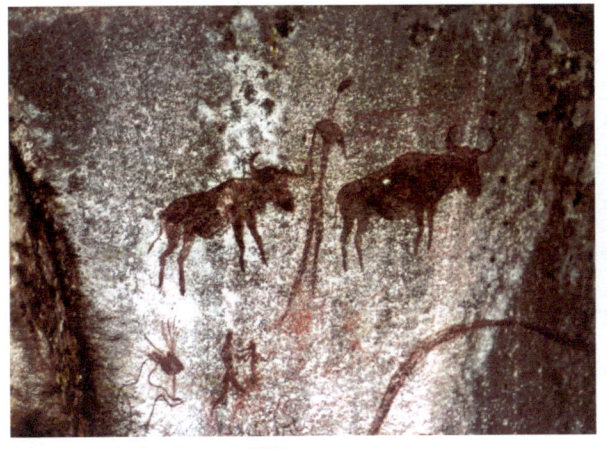

Nsangwini, circa 1955

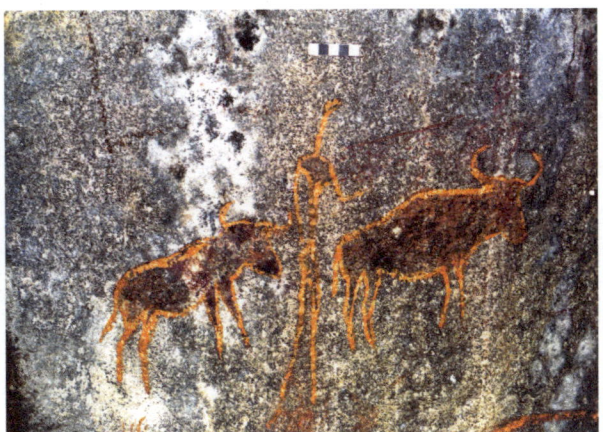

Nsangwini, circa 2000

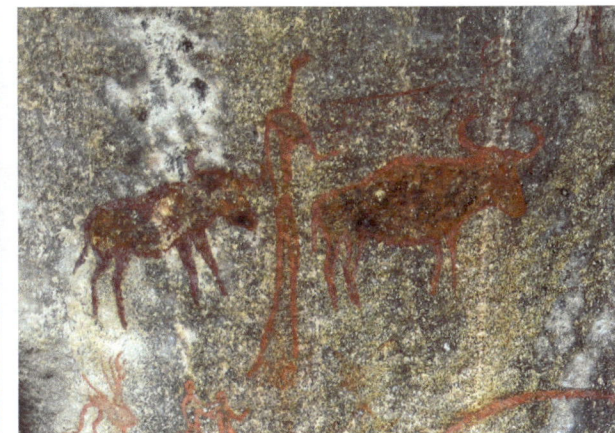

Nsangwini, circa 2020

WHY ARE MOST ROCK ART SITES SECRET?

Worldwide rock art researchers keep site locations secret. The reason is simple: most public sites are vandalised unless they are very carefully managed. The best known site in the country, Nsangwini near Maguga Dam, has been open to the public for decades.

In the 1980s visitor numbers were low and a community member decided to use washing powder on the central panel to clean it. The result would have looked good initially, water brightens paintings, but when dry they would have been duller than before. Then someone decided to outline all the central panel paintings to make them more obvious, using orange enamel paint. When rumours spread that the paintings had been vandalised visitors stopped coming.

Then, around 2004, funding from the European Union became available to create a community project around the paintings. An expert restorer from the Getty Museum in California arrived to remove the orange paint, but it had been hardened by time and intense summer heat. The enamel paint could not be removed without damaging the paintings beneath.

Removable brown acrylic paint, mixed with an invisible fluorescent dye, was carefully added over the orange enamel to tone it down. Under UV light the additions will instantly fluoresce, making the restorations obvious for future restorers.

There was a site at Sandlane open to the public, it was also touched up with orange enamel, but the paint ran over the paintings, destroying some entirely. Both sites have signs that people have tried to chip away at the paintings.

Graffiti is not a serious problem in Eswatini, but digging for gold is. There is a myth that San paintings indicate buried gold; the Kruger Millions. There is no truth behind this. President Kruger never came anywhere near the country. The digging persists though, and it destroys the archaeological context associated with paintings. One site has destructive holes so deep that large tree trunks have been lowered in as stepladders.

Recently marijuana growers have been storing their dry crop in rock shelters. If these bundles of marijuana catch light from veld fires the intense heat generated can severely damage or destroy the rock art.

41

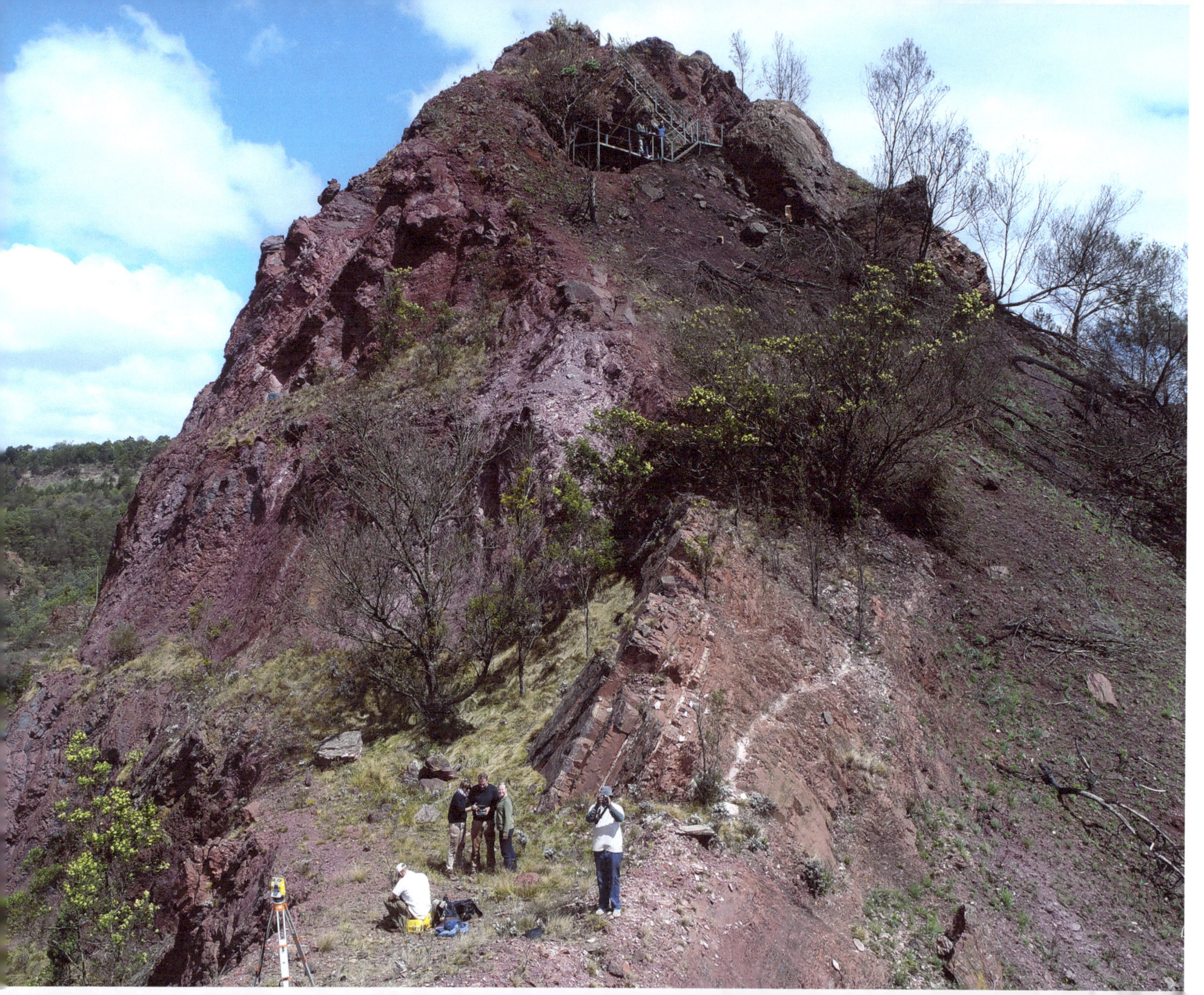

CURRENT RESEARCH

For tens of thousands of years, people climbed hundreds of metres up steep slopes to mine ochre at Lion Cavern. There was also a large ancient quarry on the mountaintop where thousands of kilograms of ore were carefully removed.

This period was in the stone ages, long before humans discovered that iron could be melted and formed into weapons and tools. So the miners were not using the ore for iron implements, there had to have been another use. Archaeologists are currently researching ochre throughout Eswatini, not just at the Ngwenya mine site. They are trying to determine where ochre samples from previous archaeological excavations countrywide were actually mined.

This is possible because each piece of ochre has a unique blend of components. These can be measured by reducing ochre to its atomic components in a nuclear reactor and then analysing the results. Samples found countrywide can then be matched to their sources, creating a map of ochre networks thousands of years old.

Archaeologists will be excavating two recently discovered ancient mines at Ngwenya, found while they were re-excavating the already well known Lion Cavern. These newly discovered mines were sliced in half by industrial iron ore mining and remained hidden in plain sight for decades. They were found by flying drones around the inaccessible cliffs in the vicinity and taking photos.

A dating technique, Optically-Stimulated Luminescence, is being used to date these. This new technology utilises a basic characteristic of many crystals; their absorption of sunlight as energy which is stored within them. This energy slowly releases at a consistent rate over time. Archaeologists can use this for dating because buried grains of sand are tiny quartz crystals - and the amount of ancient sunlight in them can be measured, grain by grain, providing timelines as to when they were buried. To be accurate, they need to be excavated in complete darkness by hammering tubes into the earth and taking core samples. These are later opened under laboratory conditions in order to be dated.

Further excavations will thoroughly analyse and date the ancient mines with funding from the German Archaeological Institute.

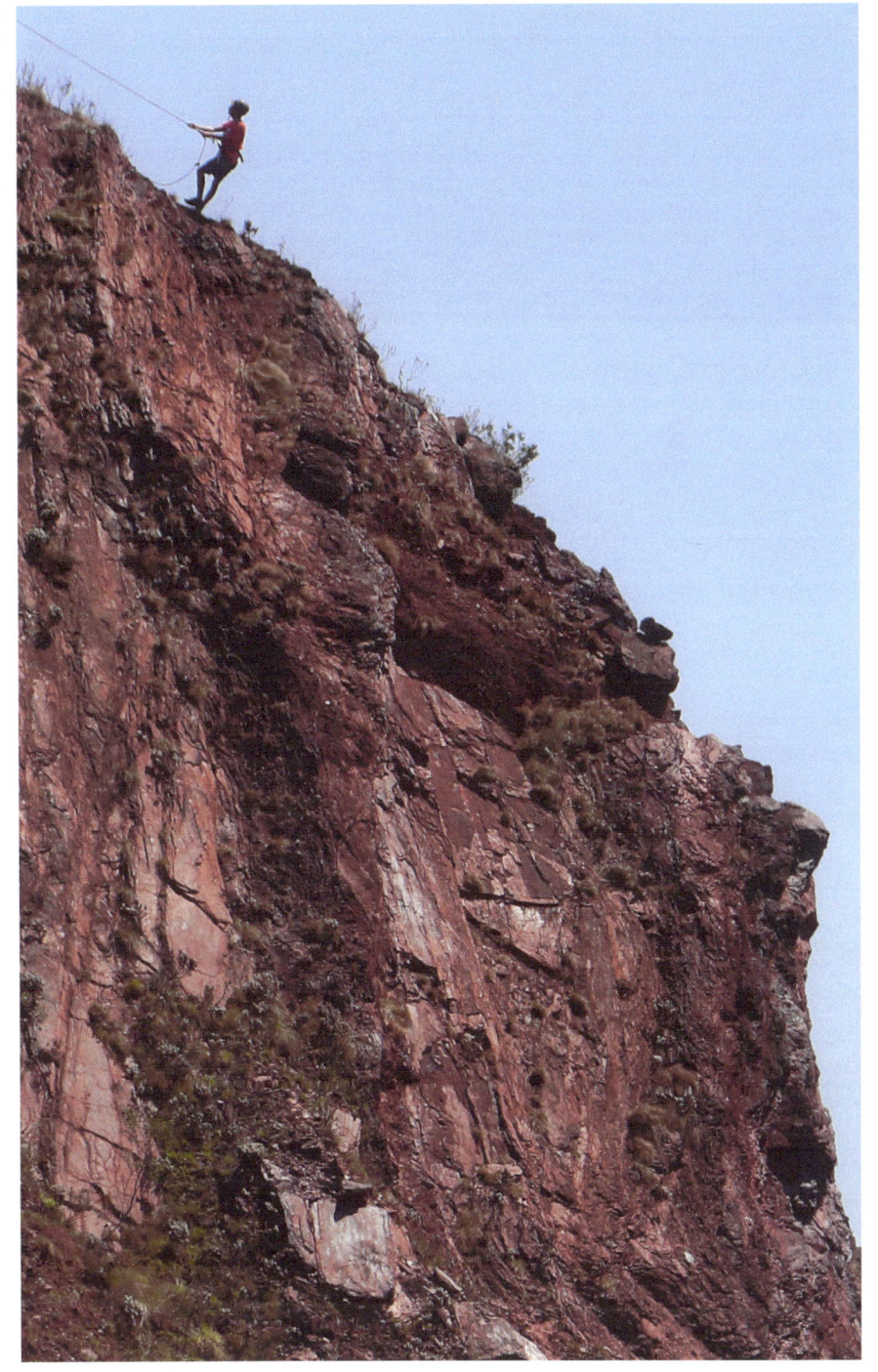

Left: Lion Cavern is accessed by a steel walkway, seen at the top of the photo. It is on the rim of the industrial iron ore mine at Ngwenya.
Right: Abseiling to obtain archaeological samples for dating.

PLACES OF INTEREST

Lion Cavern

The world's oldest known mine. Around 43 000 years ago people were mining ochre at this site, and probably used it to connect to their ancestors, as it is today across Eswatini. Ochre mining at Ngwenya has continued ever since, making it the world's longest known cultural tradition in one location. Spectacular scenery. 15 minute easy walk. Entry is through Malolotja Nature Reserve. E25 per person.
GPS 26°12'58.23"E 31°01'47.27"S

Nsangwini Community Rock Art Site

Located in a pleasant fertile rural area near Maguga Dam where one can glimpse Swazi rural life. The site is a painted granite rock shelter overlooking the scenic Komati River winding through a wild gorge. Wear walking shoes and carry a stick, the trail is steep and rocky in places. It takes about twenty minutes to go down, and thirty to come back up. Trained community guides available. Beware of intense summer heat and carry water. Approximately 4 000 years old. About E30 per person.
GPS 26°04'01.23"S 31°17'44.02"E

Ntfonjeni

The site of God's footprint in granite. Whatever one's opinion, early people accepted it as a place of great power. There is cultural continuity extending from ancient San (there is a very faint painting) through early Swazi history to the present. The royal homestead of Ntfonjeni, which guards the footprint, is close by. The site is close to the road with easy access. Approximately 4 000 years old. Entry price to be negotiated with the guide. E25 is suggested.
GPS 25°49'53.92"S 31°21'08.91"E

Mantenga Cultural Village

This recreation of a late 1800s chief's homestead is close to the main tourist area of Ezulwini. It is isolated by scenic cliffs, giving a real feeling of what life would have been like then. Guided tours and energetic Swazi cultural dancing twice a day at 11.15 AM and 3 PM. The village is within the Mantenga Nature Reserve with a peaceful river running through it, excellent birdlife, some mammals and the scenic Mantenga waterfall. There are walking trails along the river and into the surrounding mountains. Riverside accommodation and a basic restaurant. Entrance E100
GPS 26°26'48.22"S 31°09'48.51"E

Eswatini National Museum

The museum is next to Parliament in Lobamba, between Ezulwini and Malkerns. It has detailed permanent displays on Swazi traditional culture, as well as a fascinating photographic timeline from initial 19th century colonial contact to Independence. This helps visitors get a feel for how Swazi culture adapted to a vastly changing world during the colonial period. There is also a small art gallery. Entrance E80 adult - E30 children.
GPS 26°26'48.73"S 31°12'25.95"E

Mantjolo Pool

This is a highveld pool close to Mbabane in attractive rural countryside, accessible by car. You will need to use the GPS point, no signposts. The level of the pool mysteriously remains constant year round, it is sacred to the Mnisi clan who gather annually for rituals. It is a National Monument. The suggested fee per car is E25 to E30 to the custodian who may or may not appear.
GPS 26°15'51.05"S 31°07'17.66E

Bulembu Museum

Bulembu is an old mining town, once the site of 19th century gold mines and later a large asbestos mine. It is now safe to visit and has a large museum on mining and colonialism. It includes a rare and interesting 1930s cableway station that once spanned high mountain peaks. Bulembu is now the site of a large orphanage, there is a comfortable lodge in the remote town with hiking trails into the mountains. The road between Pigg's Peak and Bulembu is rough dirt. 4x4s only in wet weather. Spectacular mountain scenery.
GPS 25°57'12.28"S 31°07'38.86"E

Barberton-Makhonjwa Geotrail

Eswatini has some of the oldest rock formations worldwide at 3.5 billion years old. These formations extend across the Swati-South African border. There is a well presented geology trail with explanatory displays and examples between Barberton in South Africa and Bulembu in Eswatini. The scenery is best seen in the Bulembu to Barberton direction, but if you prioritise geology, then reversing the direction will present rocks from younger to older. A free, self-guided drive with breathtaking scenery.

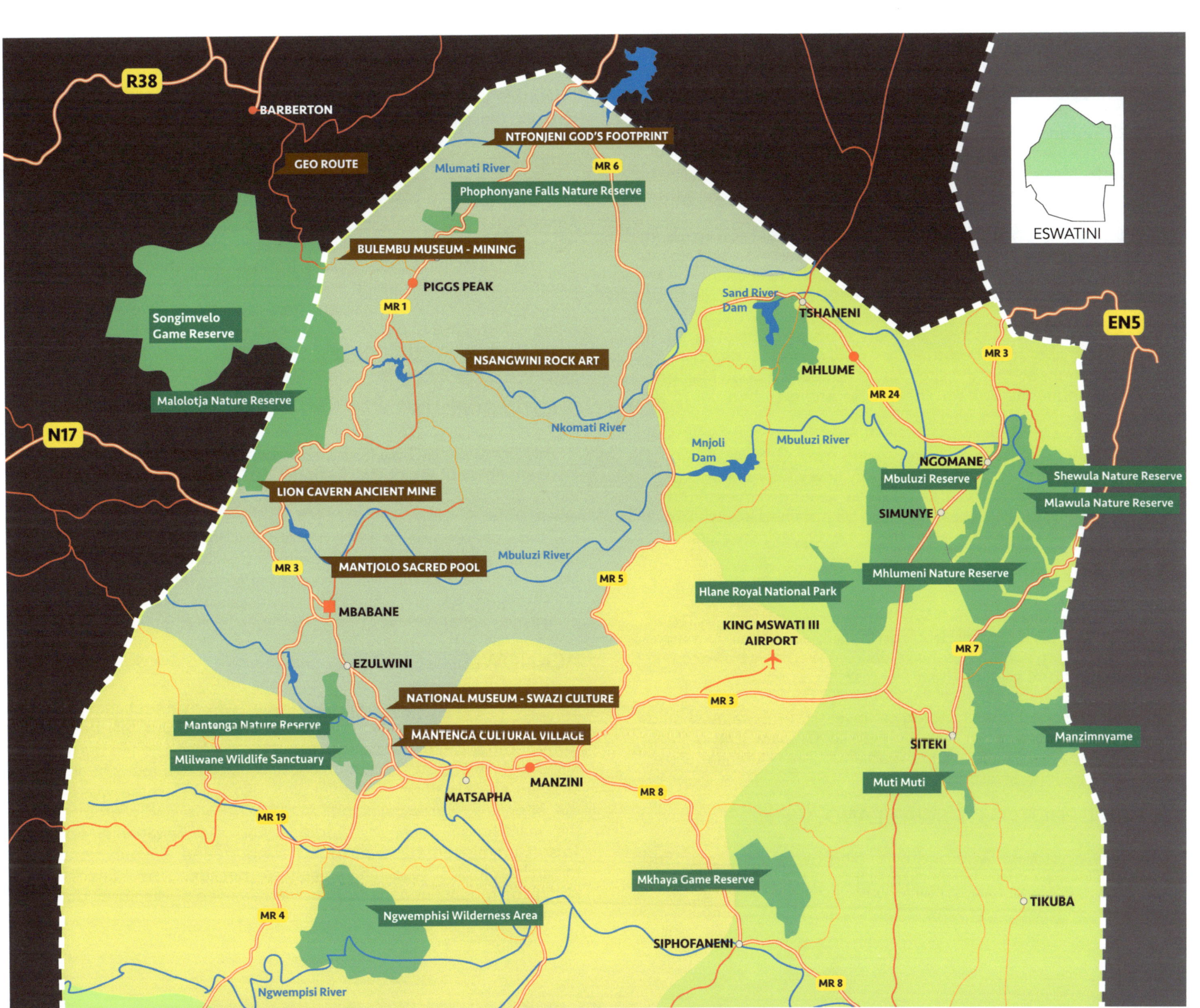

R38

BARBERTON

GEO ROUTE

Mlumati River

NTFONJENI GOD'S FOOTPRINT

MR 6

Phophonyane Falls Nature Reserve

BULEMBU MUSEUM - MINING

PIGGS PEAK

Sand River Dam

TSHANENI

EN5

MR 1

Songimvelo Game Reserve

NSANGWINI ROCK ART

MHLUME

MR 3

MR 24

Malolotja Nature Reserve

N17

Nkomati River

Mnjoli Dam

Mbuluzi River

NGOMANE

Mbuluzi Reserve

Shewula Nature Reserve

LION CAVERN ANCIENT MINE

SIMUNYE

Mlawula Nature Reserve

Mbuluzi River

MR 3

MANTJOLO SACRED POOL

MR 5

Hlane Royal National Park

Mhlumeni Nature Reserve

MBABANE

KING MSWATI III AIRPORT

EZULWINI

MR 7

NATIONAL MUSEUM - SWAZI CULTURE

MR 3

Mantenga Nature Reserve

MANTENGA CULTURAL VILLAGE

SITEKI

Manzimnyame

Mlilwane Wildlife Sanctuary

Muti Muti

MATSAPHA

MANZINI

MR 8

MR 19

MR 4

Mkhaya Game Reserve

TIKUBA

Ngwemphisi Wilderness Area

SIPHOFANENI

MR 8

Ngwempisi River

ESWATINI

HISTORY OF ROCK ART RESEARCH

Archaeological research in Eswatini began in the early 1950s when Johnny Masson and Henry Hlahlamelo Dlamini started spending weekends out in the hills searching for rock art, often sleeping in remote homesteads. Dlamini was a tax collector and knew people countrywide. Masson - an atypical colonial administrator - published several academic papers on Bushman paintings, as they were then known.

Travel was difficult at the time because there were few roads in rural areas. In the late fifties, he was provided with a Land Rover for research by the colonial administration which was headed by an anthropologist. At the time, the entire police force had three Land Rovers.

In the early 2000s Masson - by then in his late seventies - and Bob Forrester photographed the sites on film and recorded thirty one GPS locations so that the sites would not be lost upon Masson's demise. Subsequently some of the GPS locations turned out to be incorrect.

A decade later, Forrester, Mauro Almaviva, Lucky Gama and Sibusiso Dlamini redid the survey using two GPSs and digital cameras. During the second survey, twenty new sites were recorded. Most photos in this book are from the second survey. Further information for academic researchers can be obtained from the Rock Art Research Institute (RARI) at the University of the Witwatersrand.

FURTHER READING

THE ARCHAEOLOGY OF SWAZILAND: An Introduction, by JR Masson, 2011. This is the only book on the subject with an extensive section on rock art, sometimes available from Websters bookstore in Mbabane and from: shelagh@realnet.co.sz

People interested in archaeological research in Eswatini should retrieve articles through JSTOR by Fumiko Ohinata, David Price Williams, Andrew Watson, Larry Barham, Tom Huffman, Peter Beaumont and John Masson.

ARCHIVAL PHOTOS OF SWAZILAND

Historical photos of Swaziland extending back to the late 19th century can be viewed and downloaded free by Googling Swaziland Digital Archives.

FUTURE ARCHAEOLOGICAL RESEARCH

Further excavations at Ngwenya should thoroughly analyze and date the ancient mines with a grant from the Deutsche Forschungsgemeinschaft. The excavated material will be compared with ochre samples from historic archaeological excavations countrywide.

The exact composition of the ochre will be determined by the Archaeometry Laboratory at the University of Missouri Research Reactor. Samples will then be matched to their sources, creating a map of ancient ochre networks.

The German Archaeological Institute and the Senckenberg Centre for Human Evolution and Palaeontology at the University of Tuebingen are currently studying two recently discovered ancient mines at Ngwenya to obtain quartz samples for Optically-Stimulated Luminescence dating. Provisional results from the ongoing research confirm the ancient dates.

PHOTO CREDITS

All photos are by Bob Forrester, except for the following: P4 German Archaeological Institute. P10 top left, right, Masson estate. P12 internet, photographer unknown. P16 top right, Masson estate. P28, Sandy Wales. P34 left, sangoma, courtesy Steve Hall. P37 top, Joseph Raucher 1895, bottom, old postcard, photographer unknown. P41 bottom, photographer unknown. P42 top right, Masson estate. P43 left, Masson estate. P45 Eswatini map courtesy of Mbongeni Dlamini. All DStretch images by Mauro Almaviva. Swaziland Digital Archives provided the archival photos.

ACKNOWLEDGEMENTS

The Deutsches Archäologisches Institut (German Archaeological Institute) kindly sponsored the book. Jen Cowie of Chilli Pepper Consulting quickly and expertly laid out the book and edited the text. Richard Hulley kindly read the manuscript and provided thoughtful criticism as did Mlungisi Dlamini who also provided the words of the Ntonjeni regimental song. Anthony Angus kindly proofread the manuscript. Rosemary Andrade and the Eswatini National Trust Commission have provided support and encouragement for archaeological research projects for decades. The Waterford-Kamhlaba Mountaineering Club helped archaeologists abseil down the cliffs at Ngwenya to obtain samples.

Man in trance with folded wings.

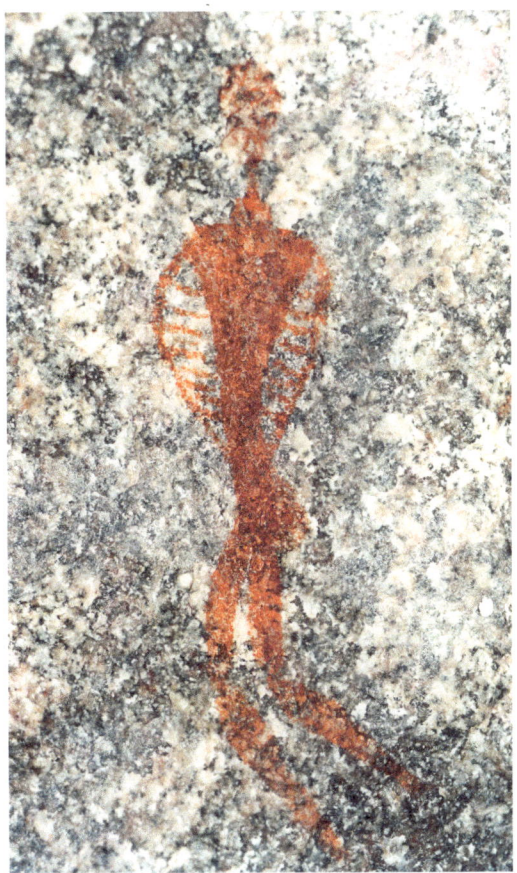

The Red Thread
Freethinkrs Press
All rights reserved, this book may not be reproduced or stored
in any media without the written permission of the publishers.
Bon Accord, Lutindzi Drive, PO Box 906, Mbabane, Eswatini
Design: Chilli Pepper Consulting
Text copyright: Bob Forrester
ISBN 978-0-7978-0567-5
Contact: bobforrester@rocketmail.com
2020

Bob Forrester is a heritage specialist who was born and grew up in Eswatini. He is the author of four books on facets of the country, and has co-authored and edited several more, including The Archaeology of Swaziland. He has designed and created four museums in the country. His book, The First People: How We Became Human, provides an innovative approach to human cultural evolution over the last 320 000 years.

Mauro Almaviva is a medical doctor who was born in Bologna, Italy. He has worked extensively in public health throughout Africa with the Italian Cooperation. His deep interest in history and archaeology resulted in him finding previously unrecorded rock art sites in Eswatini. His African travels are published in Il Cofanetto Magico, and he is the co-author of a book (in press) on the WW II defences of Alghero in Italy.

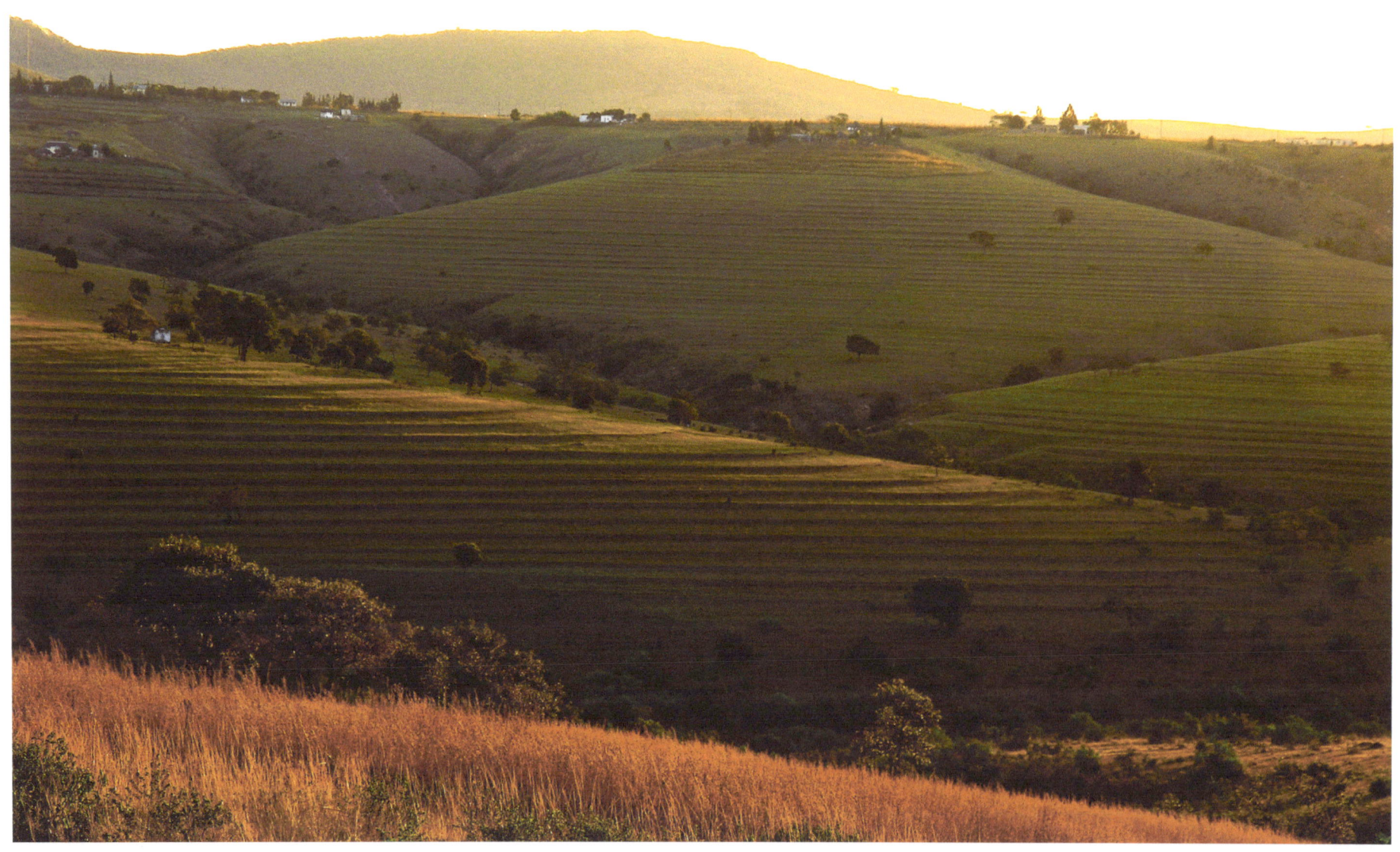

www.ingramcontent.com/pod-product-compliance
Lightning Source LLC
Chambersburg PA
CBHW041110170526
45159CB00009BA/2908